THEMATIC UNIT

Mayans, Aztecs and Incas

Written by Linda J. Larsen

Teacher Created Materials, Inc.
6421 Industry Way
Westminster, CA 92683
www.teachercreated.com

©1996 Teacher Created Materials, Inc.
Reprinted, 2001
Revised, 2001
Made in U.S.A.

ISBN 1-55734-595-3

Illustrated by
Ken Tunell

Edited by
Barbara M. Wally, M.S.

Cover Art by
Keith Vasconcelles

Table of Contents

Introduction

Mayans, Aztecs and Incas contains a captivating, whole language, thematic unit based on the pre-Columbian civilizations of Central and South America. Its pages are filled with a wide variety of lesson ideas and reproducible pages designed for use with intermediate, middle, and junior high school students. At its core are three high-quality young adult literature selections: *The Corn Grows Ripe, Aztecs: The Fall of the Aztec Capital (DK Discoveries),* and *Secret of the Andes.*

For each literature selection activities are included which set the stage for reading, encourage enjoyment of the book, and extend the concepts. The theme crosses the curriculum with activities in language arts, social studies, science, math, art, writing, architecture, and creative thinking skills. Many of these activities encourage cooperative learning. Because of the commonalities of the cultures, most of the activities may be used with any selection should you choose to read only one or two of the books.

Thematic units should be planned with an understanding of the reading activities and organizational ability of the individuals and unique group that will be participating in the unit. Some classes will take more time to cover the unit, while others will be able to do more projects independently or in cooperative learning groups.

This thematic unit includes:

❑ **literature selections**—summaries of three books with related lessons that cross the curriculum

❑ **planning guides**—suggestions for sequencing lessons and activities each day of the unit

❑ **writing ideas**—writing activities across the curriculum, including student created books

❑ **bulletin board ideas**—suggestions and plans for student-created and/or interactive bulletin boards

❑ **curriculum connections**—in language arts, poetry, math, social studies, science, architecture, life skills, games, and art

❑ **group projects**—to encourage cooperative learning

❑ **culminating activities**—which require students to synthesize their learning and create products that can be shared with others

❑ **a bibliography**—suggested additional fiction and nonfiction books, videos, computer programs, and teacher resources

---

To keep this valuable resource intact so that it can be used year after year, you may wish to punch holes in the pages and store them in a three-ring binder.

Introduction *(cont.)*

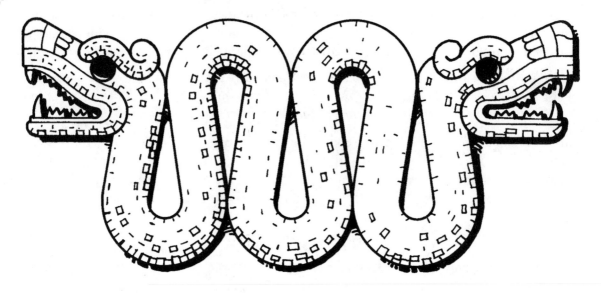

Why a Balanced Approach?

The strength of a whole language approach is that it involves children in using all modes of communication—reading, writing, listening, illustrating, and doing. Communication skills are interconnected and integrated into lessons that emphasize the whole of language. Balancing this approach is our knowledge that every whole, including individual words, is composed of parts, and directed study of those parts can help a student to master the whole. Experience and research tell us that regular attention to phonics, other word-attack skills, spelling, etc., develops reading mastery, thereby fulfilling the whole language experience. The child is thus led to read, write, spell, speak, and listen confidently in response to a literature experience introduced by the teacher. In these ways, language skills grow rapidly, stimulated by direct practice, involvement, and interest in the topic at hand.

Why Thematic Planning?

One useful tool for implementing an integrated whole language program is thematic planning. By choosing a theme with correlating literature selections for a unit of study, a teacher can plan activities throughout a day to form a cohesive, in-depth study of the topic. Students will be practicing and applying their skills in meaningful contexts. Consequently, they will tend to learn and retain more. Both teachers and students will be freed from a day that is broken into unrelated segments of isolated drill and practice.

Why Cooperative Learning?

Along with academic skills and content, students need to learn social skills. No longer can this area of development be taken for granted. Students must learn to work cooperatively in groups in order to function well in modern society. Group activities should be a regular part of school life, and teachers should consciously include social objectives as well as academic objectives in their planning. For example, a group working together to write a play may need to select a leader. The teacher should make clear to the students and monitor the qualities of good leader-follower group interaction just as he/she would state and monitor the academic goals of the project.

The Corn Grows Ripe

by Dorothy Rhoads

Summary

This Newbery Honor Book tells the story of a young Mayan boy growing up in Mexico's Yucatan peninsula. Twelve-year old Tigre must take over the family responsibilities when his father is injured. For Tigre and his family, life is a blend of ancient Mayan heritage and modern life. Illustrated in the style of ancient Mayan paintings, the story is rich in Mayan language and culture, and details the rituals and customs of daily life in a Mayan village.

The outline shown below is a suggested plan for using the various activities presented in this unit. You should adapt these ideas to fit your own classroom situation.

Sample Lesson Plan

Lesson 1
- ❏ Introduce the book, *The Corn Grows Ripe*.
- ❏ Complete one or more Setting the Stage activities, page 6.
- ❏ View a video about the Maya.
- ❏ Make paper flowers. (page 78)

Lesson 2
- ❏ Read pages 9–26.
- ❏ Choose items from Chapter Activities, pages 9–10.
- ❏ Start a dictionary mural. (See Enjoying the Book, page 7)
- ❏ Learn about the land of the Maya, pages 15–16.
- ❏ Design a Mayan glyph pendant, page 17.

Lesson 3
- ❏ Read pages 27–41.
- ❏ Choose items from Chapter Activities, pages 9–10.
- ❏ Add any new words to the dictionary mural.
- ❏ Begin the Cultural Time Line, page 60.
- ❏ Read about the rain forest and begin plans for a terrarium, pages 20–21.
- ❏ Explore Maya Math, page 57.

Lesson 4
- ❏ Read pages 42–57.
- ❏ Choose items from Chapter Activities pages 9–10.
- ❏ Add any new words to the dictionary mural.
- ❏ Continue Maya Math, pages 57–58.
- ❏ Read about the calendar round, page 18.
- ❏ Begin a pinch pot, page 70.

Lesson 5
- ❏ Read pages 58–70.
- ❏ Choose items from Chapter Activities, pages 9–10.
- ❏ Add any new words to the dictionary mural.
- ❏ Find Long Count Dates, page 19.
- ❏ Assemble a rain forest terrarium, page 21.
- ❏ Choose an item from Enjoying the Book, page 7, to complete.
- ❏ Play an ancient game, page 73.

Lesson 6
- ❏ Read pages 71–83.
- ❏ Choose items from Chapter Activities, pages 9–10.
- ❏ Finish the dictionary mural.
- ❏ Complete glyph pendant, page 17.
- ❏ Prepare Mayan food and sprout corn, pages 64–65.
- ❏ Do one or more Vocabulary Activities, pages 13–14.

Lesson 7
- ❏ Complete the Vocabulary Activities, pages 13–14.
- ❏ Choose activities from Extending the Book, page 8, to complete.
- ❏ Create pictures to add to the classroom bulletin board page 77.

Overview of Activities

Setting the Stage

1. Prepare a bulletin board to look like the rain forest, with rain forest animals and Mayan step pyramids. (See page 77)

2. Prepare a research and work area in the classroom with information, books, posters, maps, etc. about the Maya, Central America, and rain forests. A variety of artifacts suitable for classroom display are available from Ethnic Arts and Facts (see bibliography). Encourage students to bring in items to share or display, like postcards, stamps, magazines, pictures, serapes, corn products, coins, etc.

3. In 1995 and again in 1996, Dan Buettner led a team of explorers in "Maya Quest." The participants rode bicycles through the jungles, looking for answers to questions about the "mysterious Maya." Their journey was directed by students in classrooms throughout the world by way of computers. Interactive technology allowed students to be "present" in real time for the opening of new sites and to contribute their insights to the interpretation of newly revealed glyphs. Archives and information about the discoveries, lesson plans, projects, and references to other Maya sites on the Internet may be accessed at **http://mayaquest.mecc.com./mayaquest.html**

4. The mystery of the Maya has puzzled and challenged archaeologists and explorers for centuries. Several videos of recent explorations are available. Show one or more to acquaint students with the terrain and culture of the Maya.

5. Begin a time line (page 60) to show the origins, growth, and decline of Central and South American cultures. Include key facts about historic events in other parts of the world, like Europe and Asia, for comparison.

6. Locate Central America on a world map. Ask students to complete the map activities on pages 15–16. Make two transparencies for the overhead projector. On the first, show the location of Classic Maya centers, physical features, and rain forest areas. Use the second copy as an overlay. Use different colors to indicate modern cities, current rain forest areas, etc.

7. Planting a garden was very important to the Maya. Divide the class into groups. Give each group an egg carton. Fill each section with potting soil. Plant a different vegetable seed in each section. Make a location chart on the lid of the egg carton. While you study the Maya, compare and graph how the different seeds grow.

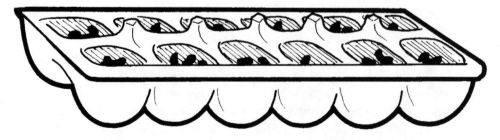

8. The story starts with a Mayan myth about the creation of the human race. Read creation myths of other cultures, like Egyptian, Roman, Viking, or Native American, and discuss the similarities and the differences. Create a class book illustrating these different versions.

Overview of Activities *(cont.)*

Enjoying the Book

1. Assign pages for reading each day. See the Sample Lesson Plan on page 5 for suggestions. Chapter Activities, pages 9–12, provide questions to direct the reading and critical thinking processes, hands-on activities related to each day's assignment, and critical vocabulary.

2. Make a dictionary mural. Divide a long strip of butcher paper into 26 sections and label the top of each section with a letter of the alphabet. As the students complete their reading assignment each day, have them write in the Mayan and Spanish words from the story under the appropriate letter and add the English translations. Encourage the students to use these words in their writing. Add any other Spanish words they want to record.

3. The Maya developed a written language based on glyphs. Early scholars thought that these picture writings concerned only astronomy. Current researchers are using computer technology to decode the complex records left by the Maya as part of their monuments. Have students create individual glyphs, page 17, to make pendants and stelae.

4. Look closely at the illustrations in the book or from other sources. The Maya are shown with sloping foreheads, which, along with crossed eyes, were considered highly attractive and desirable. Mothers bound boards on infants' foreheads to encourage this sloping look and tied beads between the infants' eyes to cause them to cross. As a class, discuss how attitudes toward attractiveness have changed. What is considered attractive now?

5. Plant a rain forest terrarium, page 21, to observe how plants interact in this unique ecosystem.

6. Read *The Great Kapok Tree* by Lynn Cherry (HBJ, 1990) to learn more about the rain forest. Create a display of rain forest plants, animals, and products.

7. The ancient Maya were very concerned with the passage of time and worked out a system of dating events in their world, known as The Long Count. It is these dates that have finally permitted scientists to begin decoding the complex riddle of the Mayan civilization. Read page 19 and help students translate their birthdays to Long Count dates.

8. Have the students draw people, animals, and objects from the story. Add these to the Mayan bulletin board. Use your completed dictionary mural to play word games like hangman or bingo. Create poetry, using new words. Have the students write the Spanish words vertically down the paper and English words to describe those words horizontally. Add designs and color.

Overview of Activities *(cont.)*

Extending the Book

1. The ancient Maya were one of the few cultures to understand and use the concept of zero in mathematics. Use the activities on pages 57 and 58 to introduce students to the vigesimal (base 20) system used by the Maya. Key math concepts, including place value, can be reinforced by exploring other numerical systems. For more activities, *Maya Math* from Sunburst Communications provides detailed lesson plans, worksheets and computer support. In addition, the Glyph Trek section allows students to apply Mayan numbers to solve puzzles, and a calendar calculates Mayan Long Count Dates. The computerized calculator permits students to explore other numerical bases.

2. The best known application of Mayan mathematics is in the area of calendaring. The Calendar Round predates the Maya and was used by the Aztecs, as well. Read page 18 to learn more about this calendar system.

3. Celebrate with a corn festival. Bring in foods made from corn products. Listen to music. Tell corny jokes. Have a piñata. Let the students brainstorm ideas for corny activities and organize their own festival.

4. Start a school-wide recycling of aluminum cans. Use the money to adopt rain forest acres in Central America. For more information, contact one of the following organizations

   The Nature Conservancy   or   **National Arbor Day Foundation**
   1-800-628-6860   *1-800-255-5500*

5. Read books and stories about the Maya.

Factual:	*The Maya* by Jacqueline D. Greene (Franklin Watts)
Contemporary:	"A Clown's Story" by Mario Bencastro from the Latin American short story collection for students, *Where Angels Glide at Dawn* (Harper Trophy)
Legend:	*The Hummingbird King* by Argentina Placios (Troll Associates)

6. There are many theories about why the Mayan culture was so advanced. Some people believe that the Maya came from the lost continent of Atlantis, while others propose that the Maya and the Egyptians shared a common origin. Make a list of commonalities like pyramids, glyphs, etc. Have students present a debate on the topic "The Maya Originated in Egypt."

7. Although they abandoned the great cities, the Maya have not disappeared. Lacandon Mayas continue to live a traditional lifestyle in the tropical rain forests of Mexico. In recent years, many Maya have been victims of civil unrest in Central America. In 1992, Rigoberta Menchu, a Mayan woman from Guatemala, received the Nobel Peace Prize for her efforts in resolving the tensions. Students can learn more about modern Mayan life from her autobiography *I . . . Rigoberta Menchu: An Indian Woman In Guatemala* (Routledge, Chapman & Hall)

Chapter Activities

Foreword *(pages 9–12)*

For Discussion: According to the Mayan folk tale, humans were created from mud, then wood, and finally from corn. Write all three materials on the board and discuss the pros and cons of each.

Activity: Choose a modern material like plastic or aluminum. Write a folk tale telling how people were created from that material.

Foreign Vocabulary: *milpas* (cornfields), *milpa* (preparing the land), *metates* (stone grinders), *tortillas* (corn pancakes), *atole* (a corn and water drink)

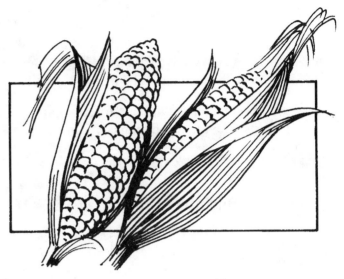

Chapter 1—"The Family" *(pages 15–20)*

For Discussion: a. Why does Dionisio have two names? What are they? b. List and describe the members of Tigre's family. c. What is "the bush"? What good and bad things does it provide?

Activity: Make tissue paper flowers to decorate the classroom. (See page 78.)

Foreign Vocabulary: *chachalacas* (a noisy bird), *pich* (a singing bird), *guano* (a palm tree), *mamich* (little old grandmother), *calabaza* (a bottle made from a gourd), *masa* (a corn and water dough)

Chapter 2—"The Milpa" *(pages 21–26)*

For Discussion: a. How does Tigre feel when he sees the ruins of the temple? What omen does he discover? b. It takes much effort for Tigre and his father to clear the field. Can you think of an activity where you worked really hard but did not seem to get anywhere?

Activity: List all the animals mentioned in the chapter. List all the animals that live in your local area. Compare the two lists.

Foreign Vocabulary: *curva* (a knife with a curved blade), *on* (avocado tree), *pozole* (a drink made from cornmeal and water)

Chapter 3—"Trouble" *(pages 27–30)*

For Discussion: a. Why does Tigre ache? Can you remember when you did an activity that caused you to ache? b. What do you think a bonesetter does? How do we treat broken bones differently today?

Activity: Tigre's great-grandmother's opinion of him has changed from the beginning of the story. Make a list of examples or comments from the book to prove this change.

Foreign Vocabulary: *roble* (oak tree), *anona* (a tropical fruit tree)

Chapter Activities *(cont.)*

Chapter 4—"The Journey" *(pages 31–36)*

For Discussion: a. When he hears the night noises, Tigre becomes frightened and imagines spirits are stalking him. What real nocturnal rain forest animals do you think the Snake Witch, the giant Juan, the Palm-Leaf-Mat Witch and Xtabai are? Have you ever been in a situation where natural noises seemed scary? b. Why is Tigre taking a chicken and a pot of honey with him? Discuss the concept of bartering.

Activity: Draw a picture of the rain forest showing either the real nocturnal animals or Tigre's imagined spirits in crayon, and then cover the picture with a black wash of paint.

Foreign Vocabulary: *santo* (the image of a saint), *ceiba* (the kapok tree)

Chapter 5—"Bushing Milpa" *(pages 37–41)*

For Discussion: a. If the students in Tigre's village school fail, the parents must pay a fine. How is this different from your school? b. Why does Tigre decide to plant more corn?

Activity: If you were in charge of planting crops, what would you plant? How could you make a profit? Why would you choose certain crops? Draw a design for your farm and write a paragraph explaining your decisions.

Foreign Vocabulary: *Ai,* (an exclamation like Ah!), *tzoki* (an expression—it is finished)

Chapter 6—"Study" *(pages 42–46)*

For Discussion: a. The medicine man uses anona leaves, honey and garlic as a remedy. What would a doctor prescribe? Can you think of some other folk remedies? b. Don Alfonso and Tigre's great-grandmother disagree about the fire. What advice does Don Alfonso give Tigre? How does this help him solve the problem of the vampire bat?

Activities: 1. Research vampire bats or other species of bats. Draw a picture, then write a paragraph explaining some important facts. Share your information with the class.
2. Research medicines that have come from folk medicine, like quinine, curare and hydrocortisone. Tell where they are found in nature and what they are used for.

Chapter 7—"Burning Milpa" *(pages 47–52)*

For Discussion: a. What is the process that Tigre goes through to "light the field"? b. How does he look and feel as he walks home? When have you felt proud about something you accomplished?

Activity: Have a whistling contest.

Foreign Vocabulary: *ramon* (a tree), *manhache* (a strong rain), *catzim* (a small, spiny tree)

Chapter Activities *(cont.)*

Chapter 8—"Anticipation"
(pages 53–57)

For Discussion: a. Why does Tigre think that they will have a good harvest? b. What two events will take place in May? c. Bullfights are controversial. Why is the village *corrida* different from most bullfights? d. Can you think of other feats with animals that are tests of courage?

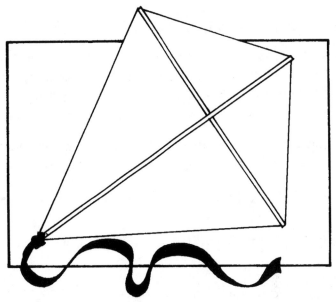

Activities: 1. Use large grocery bags and string to make kites. Have a kite flying festival. Give students five lengths of yarn each and challenge them to make ropes. Display and judge the ropes after reading Chapter 9. 2. Look up facts about ancient and modern bullfights and the running of the bulls.

Foreign Vocabulary: *corrida* (bullfight), *vaqueros* (men who lead the bulls to the ring and test their strength and courage), *sosquil* (fiber from the agave plant), *yuc* (a small deer)

Chapter 9—"The Fiesta" *(pages 58–62)*

For Discussion: Describe the sights and sounds of the fiesta. Continue discussing bullfights. Compare ancient bullfights, modern bullfights, and the running of the bulls. List pros and cons for each type of bullfight or have a debate.

Activities: 1. Judge the rope making contest. 2. Try out other types of knot tying, macramé, or different types of braids.

Foreign Vocabulary: *huipil* (native woman's dress), *vigil* (ceremonies where vaqueros must stay awake for a long time), *bravo* (well done!)

Chapter 10—"Planting" *(pages 63–65)*

For Discussion: What does Tigre plant? What planting technique does he use?

Activity: Plant a corn seed in a paper cup. Keep a graph of how much it grows in 4–6 weeks. (If you soak the seeds overnight first, they will sprout sooner.)

Chapter 11—"Hetz Mek" *(pages 66–70)*

For Discussion: a. Why is the number four important for boys and the number three important for girls? Can you think of any numbers that affect you or are considered important today? b. What does Grandfather give Tigre? Why does Grandfather think Tigre should have it?

Activity: List the nine items needed during the ceremony and explain why each is important. Imagine that the ceremony is for someone in your family. List nine items that the person will need during his/her life and explain why those items are important. Compare the two lists.

Foreign Vocabulary: *hetz mek* (a ceremony to celebrate a baby being carried on the hip), *koben* (a hearth or cooking area), *padrinos* (godparents)

Chapter Activities *(cont.)*

Chapter 12—"Drought" *(pages 71–75)*

For Discussion: a. Why is everyone worried about the lack of rain? Has your local area ever been affected by drought? b. How do the people of the village ask for rain? What is Mamich's explanation of the drought? What happened when she was young?

Activity: Purchase two small plants. In class, water one regularly and let the second go dry, as in drought conditions. In about two to three weeks, uproot the plants and examine them. Make a comparison chart or diagram of your findings.

Foreign Vocabulary: *novenario* (a public religious ceremony over nine days)

Chapter 13—"Chac Chac" *(pages 76–79)*

For Discussion: a. Why do the villagers think a ceremony is necessary? b. Why do the boys represent frogs instead of a different animal?

Activity: Research some of the unusual tree frogs found in the rain forest. Draw a picture of one and write a paragraph about some important facts. Display and share your information with the class.

Foreign Vocabulary: *Chac Chac* (the rain ceremony), *balche* (a drink made from bark and honey), *lelem* (a machete used by the gods to create lightening)

Chapter 14—"The Rains Come" *(pages 80–81)*

For Discussion: What are the Sprinklers and Kunku Chac? What do they represent?

Activity: Fold a piece of drawing paper into thirds. On the first ⅓, draw what your local area would look like in a drought, in the middle ⅓, draw what it would look like in the regular season, and in the last ⅓, draw what it would look like in a flood. How do you think your area is different from Tigre's environment?

Chapter 15—"Harvest" *(pages 82–83)*

For Discussion: Compare how you think Tigre and his father each felt at the end of the book.

Activity: Celebrate the end of the book by having a class treat—corn on the cob.

Foreign Vocabulary: *pibil nal* (roasted ears of corn)

Vocabulary Activities

As foreign words are introduced, write each one in the appropriate category. Add a definition.

Food/Drinks	Plants	Tools/Weapons	People	Miscellaneous

Extension: Make a three column chart. Label the columns Spanish, Mayan and Mexican. Try to determine the origin of each word and write it in the appropriate column.

Word Search

Find the 25 words from the list in the word search.

```
                  O L S
              I E M A A
          R L A S L N P
        A O N A M L O L L
      N Z H M I Y I N M I I
    E O A T Z U Z T A V E B M
  V P C B T C O R R I D A T I E
O B H R A M O N S O N I R D A P L
N D E H C L A B L I T V I G I L T Q E
S O R E U Q A V Y C E I B A Y N Y F E C L
G U A N O W X C U R V A L O W R C U X F S A K
D A T O L E F B H X Q E L Y X N E B O K H X N I T
```

anona	catzim	koben	milpas	ramon
atole	ceiba	lelem	novenario	tortillas
balche	corrida	manhache	padrinos	vaqueros
bravo	curva	masa	pibil nal	vigil
calabaza	guano	metates	pozole	yuc

Vocabulary Activities *(cont.)*

Match each word to its English translation. Write the correct letter next to the number.

1. _____ *anona*   a. cornfields
2. _____ *atole*   b. stone grinders
3. _____ *balche*   c. corn pancakes
4. _____ *bravo*   d. a corn and water drink
5. _____ *calabaza*   e. a palm tree
6. _____ *catzim*   f. a bottle made from a gourd
7. _____ *ceiba*   g. a corn and water dough
8. _____ *corrida*   h. a knife with a curved blade
9. _____ *curva*   i. a drink made from cornmeal and water
10. _____ *guano*   j. a tropical fruit tree
11. _____ *koben*   k. the kapok tree
12. _____ *lelem*   l. a tree
13. _____ *manhache*   m. a strong rain
14. _____ *masa*   n. a small, spiny tree
15. _____ *metates*   o. a bullfight
16. _____ *milpas*   p. men who lead the bulls to the ring and test their strength
17. _____ *novenario* q. a small deer
18. _____ *padrinos*   r. ceremony in which vaqueros must stay awake for a prolonged time
19. _____ *pibil nal* s. an expression meaning "well done"
20. _____ *pozole*   t. a hearth
21. _____ *ramon*   u. godparents
22. _____ *tortillas* v. a public religious ceremony
23. _____ *vaqueros*   w. a drink made from bark and honey
24. _____ *vigil*   x. a machete or large knife
25. _____ *yuc*   y. roasted ears of corn

On the back of this paper, write sentences using the words from the puzzle. **Example:** The *manhache* provided water for the *catzim* and the *ceiba* trees to grow.

The Land of the Maya

The remains of the great Mayan civilization are found in the Central American countries of Mexico, El Salvador, Honduras, Guatemala, and Belize. This Mayan homeland encompasses one of the most varied environments on earth. The Northern lowlands are flat, and there is little surface water, while the Southern lowlands and the volcanic highlands are rain forests.

Archaeologists believe that the earliest Maya were nomads who hunted, fished, and gathered nuts, berries, and seeds for food. By the Preclassic or Formative Period (2000 BC to AD 250), the Maya had settled in communities or villages and were farmers. Deep in the tropical rain forests, the Maya cleared the dense bush and planted corn and other crops.

In the Classic Maya Period, from A.D. 250 to 900, the Maya created a remarkable civilization. Civilization first flourished in the forested areas of Peten, where many cities like Tikal, Copan, and Palenque, each ruled by a warrior king, were built. Later, in the semiarid lands of the northern Yucatan, Uxmal, Kabah, Coba, Old Chichen, and other centers were constructed. The Maya used their incredible skill in mathematics and astronomy to build monuments and temples, calculate time, and record historic events. Drainage systems, roads, reservoirs called *chultunes,* aqueducts, and bridges contributed to life in Mayan cities.

Beginning about A.D. 800, the Maya abandoned their large lowland cities. Archaeologists have been unable to explain why this happened, but there are several theories, including war with Mexican (Toltec) armies, changes in climate, economic problems, famine, and overpopulation. The surviving people moved into the jungle where they lived in small villages. In the Postclassic Period A.D. 900–1500, the Maya in the Yucatan blended their culture with that of Toltec invaders from Central Mexico.

The first encounter with Spanish explorers was a peaceful one with Christopher Columbus in 1502. Later Spanish explorers believed they had found El Dorado, a legendary city of great wealth. The Spanish conquered and enslaved the native people. Warfare and European diseases brought by the Spanish killed as many as 90% of the Maya. Missionaries tried to convert the Maya to Christianity.

Today, all that remains of this amazing civilization are astounding temples and magnificent cities of ruins scattered throughout Central America. Descendants of the Maya live in large cities and in rural villages. Many ancient traditions of the Maya, including planting, weaving, and the use of the calendar, coexist with modern technology.

The Land of the Maya *(cont.)*

Use maps, atlases, and resource books to complete the following map activities.

Mexico

⊛ National Capital
Leon • City
—— Internaional Boundary
—— State (estado) Boundary
Jalisco State (estado) Name

200 km
0   200 Miles

1. Locate and label these bodies of water: Pacific Ocean, Caribbean Sea, Gulf of Mexico, the Gulf of California.

2. Locate these ancient cities: Tulum, Chichen Itza, Tikal, Palenque, Copan, and Utatlan.

3. Draw in and label the following: Maya Mountains, the Yucatan Peninsula, Lago de Izabel (lake), and the rain forests that existed then.

4. Shade in the areas representing the Mayan Empire.

5. On another sheet of paper, trace the map of Central America. Draw in the boundaries of the countries that exist there today. Label these countries and find their capital cities. Add the rain forests that exist today.

6. Compare the ancient and the modern maps. What is the same? What is different?

Extension: Enlarge the map and use clay, plaster of Paris, or papier mâché to create a relief map, showing the differences in terrain. Add color and texture to represent vegetation.

Mayan Glyphs

The Maya had the most advanced system of written language of all the native American groups. They used a complex form of picture writing, or hieroglyphics, in which symbols represented objects, actions, ideas, or syllables. In this way, they could write complete sentences. Scribes carved glyphs in limestone or on shells or jade. They also created books, called *codices* (singular: *codex*).

Although there were probably hundreds of codices about ceremonies, calendars, customs, literature, and science, only three have survived. An early Spanish missionary, Diego de Landa, tried to understand the Maya and sought to translate Maya writings. When the Maya refused to give up their beliefs, Landa became angry and ordered the manuscripts burned.

Fortunately, the Maya left a record of their civilization in the many glyphs carved on the steps of pyramids and other buildings and painted on murals. The Hieroglyphic Stairway at Copan contains over two thousand stones, each carved with a glyph. Stone monuments called *stelae* recorded important events in the lives of leaders. Many of these amazing monuments were hidden by the fast growing rain forest.

Archaeologists began exploring the Maya ruins in the 1800s, but it has taken over 100 years to begin to decode the Maya glyphs. As these glyphs are decoded, they reveal details of pre-Columbian life, culture, and history.

One key to understanding Maya inscriptions is the use of certain symbols to name important people, gods, and cities. Below are some examples of Maya glyphs. What glyph would you use for yourself? Choose one, or design your own symbol to tell others about yourself. Write several sentences to explain why this glyph represents you, and then make a glyph pendant.

Glyph Pendant

Materials: self hardening clay, craft sticks, dull pencils, paint

Directions:

1. Pat or roll a small amount of clay into a 2" x 5" rectangle (5 cm x 12.5 cm), ¼ inch (.63 cm) thick.

2. Use dull pencils and/or craft sticks to trace your glyph pattern into the clay. Make a hole at the top for threading the pendant on a cord.

3. Paint the clay after it has been allowed to dry. String it on a piece of string or yarn and wear it for good luck.

The Calendar Round

Time and the measurement of time were very important to the people of Central America. The calendars used by the Maya, and later the Aztecs, originated with earlier people of Mesoamerica. By observing the movement of the sun, moon, and visible planets and recording the information, the Maya calculated the length of the solar year as 365.2420 days. Modern science has measured the solar year as exactly 365.2422 days.

The first calendar was a ritual calendar called *Tzolkin*. This calendar determined ceremonial occasions. Children were named according to the day of the sacred calendar on which they were born, protected by the god of that day and governed by the omens and luck it carried. The 260 days of this sacred calendar consisted of a number (1–13) combined with a day name. The number wheel revolved inside the day name wheel so that *2 Ik* (Wind) followed *1 Imix* (Water lily). Since there were more day names than numbers, *1 Ix* (Jaguar) followed *13 Ben* (Cornstalk).

The second calendar, called the *Haab*, is a natural calendar based on the solar year. This calendar was divided into 18 months of 20 days each. The five days that remained were called *Uayeb* and did not have names. These days were considered unlucky. This natural calendar governed the agricultural seasons of the year and daily activities like planting and harvesting.

Linking the *Tzolkin* and the *Haab* like interlocking cog wheels created the Calendar Round. Each day had a name and number from each of the calendars. As an example, *1 Imix 0 Pohp* (mat) was followed by *2 Ik 1 Poph*. These particular combinations of Tzolkin day names and numbers and Haab day names and numbers would not occur again for 52 years. At the end of that time, the count would begin again, like a century in our calendar system.

Long Count Dates

Besides the calendars based on solar and lunar observations used by other Mesoamericans, the Maya developed a third method of measuring time, called the Long Count. Long Count dates appear as part of many Mayan inscriptions and have been valuable in decoding the glyphs of the Maya. By studying inscriptions, archaeologists have calculated that August 13, 3114 BC is the beginning date of this calendar. Although no one is sure exactly what this date represents, scholars think that it is the date the Maya gave for the beginning of this cycle of creation. Each event in the Maya world is recorded as the number of days that have passed since that initial date. Today, Mayan daykeepers in the mountains of Honduras maintain the ancient count and predict that this cycle of the universe will end on December 23, 2012.

Cycles of the Maya Long Count			Modern Calendar		
baktun	20 katuns	144,000 days	century	10 decades	36,525 days
katun	20 tuns	7,200 days	decade	10 years	3,652 days
tun	18 uinals	360 days	year		365 days
uinals	20 kins	20 days	month		28, 29, 30, or 31 days
kins		1 day	day		1 day

Look at the stelae below. Each shows an important date as it would appear in the Long count calendar. Use multiplication and addition to learn how many days each date represents.

October 12, 1492   **July 4, 1776**

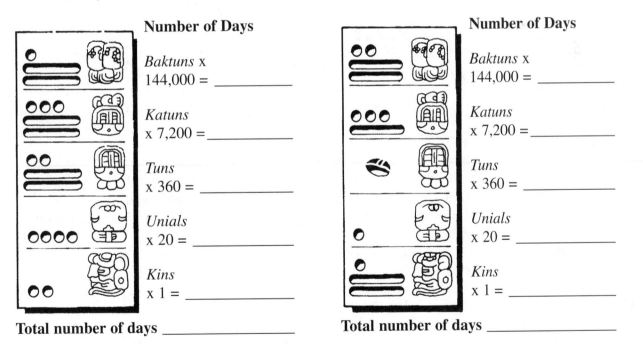

Number of Days

Baktuns x 144,000 = _____

Katuns x 7,200 = _____

Tuns x 360 = _____

Unials x 20 = _____

Kins x 1 = _____

Number of Days

Baktuns x 144,000 = _____

Katuns x 7,200 = _____

Tuns x 360 = _____

Unials x 20 = _____

Kins x 1 = _____

Total number of days _____   **Total number of days** _____

Extension: Use a computer program, or addition and subtraction, to calculate your birthday in Long Count. Add your name glyph and the glyphs for mother and father, along with a glyph to represent each parent.

The Tropical Rain Forest

Tropical rain forests are located around the middle of the Earth, between the Tropic of Cancer and the Tropic of Capricorn. In this zone, the sun is almost directly overhead, and generates more heat and solar energy than anywhere else on earth. Rainfall varies between 80 inches (2 m) and 320 inches (8 m) per year, and may be continuous or seasonal. These rain forests, or jungles, are complex and diverse ecosystems that preserve ancient life forms and serve as a source for new species of plants and animals. More than half of all the plants and animals on earth are at home in the rain forest. Many rain forest life forms have not been identified.

Vegetation in the rain forest is divided into three layers, each of which provides a variety of natural environments for plants and animals.

The top layer is the canopy, a ceiling formed by the tops of the tallest trees, which may reach 160–220 feet (49–67 m) in height. Vines and plants called epiphytes "hitchhike" on these great trees, and birds, insects, tree frogs, monkeys, and snakes live in the canopy. The canopy absorbs most of the sunlight and acts as an umbrella.

The understory contains ferns, shrubs, and dwarf trees that have adapted to the high humidity and low light conditions. In the understory, young trees grow toward the canopy, where they will replace trees that have fallen. A variety of insects and bats make their homes in the understory, and meat-eating cats lurk in the branches of the trees.

Because the soil of the rain forest contains few nutrients to support plant life, the floor of the rain forest is relatively open. Here, fungi, ants, and termites speed the decomposition of forest debris which is then recycled by the shallow-rooted trees.

Destruction of the rain forest begins with road construction. Loggers, who select and cut mahogany and tropical cedar trees for their valuable timber build most of the roads in the Central American jungle. The logging operation itself destroys an average of 17 trees for each tree harvested. When the loggers leave, landless farmers may clear what remains and plant their crops. In a few years, when the soil is depleted, the farmers move on and the land is often sold to cattle ranchers. When the grazing cattle have depleted what remained of the soil, the ranchers move on as well.

The Central American rain forest once covered 160,000 square miles (414,000 square kilometers). Today, less than 50,000 square miles (130,000 square kilometers), or about $\frac{1}{3}$ of the original rain forest, is still standing.

Activities

1. Prepare a display of rain forest plants, animals, and products.

2. Make a list of ways that you benefit from the rain forest.

The Tropical Rain Forest *(cont.)*

You can create a rain forest environment in a classroom terrarium.

Materials: five or ten gallon aquarium with a glass or clear plastic cover, gravel, ground charcoal, peat-based compost, variety of specimen plants (Refer to the list below or ask students to collect plants and seedlings from their yards.)

- **Sunplants:** marantas, dracenas, ficus, palms, rubber tree, dieffenbachia

- **Shade plants:** fittonia, peperomia, spathyphyllum

- **Epiphytes:** tillandsia, vriesia

- **Vines:** philodendron, spiderwort

Directions: Decide what to plant in the terrarium and the best planting plan. Light-tolerant plants should be taller than the shade plants and placed to represent the canopy layer of the rain forest.

1. Clean the bottom and sides of the aquarium.

2. Place a layer of gravel in the bottom of the container. Next spread charcoal over the gravel. The charcoal will act as a filter. Last, spread the planting medium over the charcoal.

3. Plant the lower, understory plants first; then, add the taller plants. If you are using epiphytes like bromeliads and climbing vines, provide some branches to support them. To plant one air plant, pack the roots of the plant in sphagnum moss. Press the root bundle into a fork or hole in the branch or tie it to a branch.

4. Mist the plants lightly with distilled water or rainwater, and cover the aquarium.

Place the aquarium in a warm, sunny area of the classroom. Within a few days you will notice drops of water collecting inside the top. This means that the ecosystem is functioning and that the water and air are cycling just the way they would in a rain forest.

Individual Terrariums

To make individual terrariums, use clear two-liter soda bottles. Carefully remove the opaque base of each bottle, and follow the directions above for planting. Cut the bottle below the neck, making sure that it is taller than the tallest plant. Place the cut end in the base, forming a dome over the terrarium.

Aztecs:
The Fall of the Aztec Capital

(DK Discoveries)

by Richard Platt

Summary

This beautifully illustrated book presents information about the history of the Aztec people and their way of life. The first section focuses on the Spanish conquest and the siege of Tenochtitlán. The remainder of the book explains the religion, diet, homes, crafts, education, and rulers of a very structured Aztec society.

Sample Lesson Plan

Lesson 1

❑ Complete Setting the Stage activity #2, page 23.

❑ Introduce information on the Aztecs and Mexico. Share stories, books, and music. (See Setting the Stage, page 23.)

❑ Learn about The Aztec's Journey and complete the Map Activities on pages 26 and 27.

❑ Make an Aztec calendar stone, page 29.

Lesson 2

❑ Add Aztec dates to the Cultural Time Line, page 60.

❑ Read *Aztecs: The Fall of the Aztec Capital*, pages 6–25.

❑ Complete the Aztec Who's Who activity, pages 33–34.

❑ Choose activities from Enjoying the Book, page 23.

❑ Create an Aztec battle shield, page 59.

Lesson 3

❑ Read pages 26–47 in *Aztecs: The Fall of the Aztec Capital*.

❑ Create a chart showing the structure of Aztec society using pages 34 and 35 in the book as a reference.

❑ Complete Enjoying the Book activity #3, page 23.

❑ Make Aztec codices, page 28.

❑ Distribute The Emperor's Zoo (page 30) and begin doing research on animals (page 31).

Lesson 4

❑ Choose one or more of the Vocabulary Activities, page 25.

❑ Choose some activities from Enjoying the Book, pages 23–24.

❑ Write pyramid poetry, pages 55–56.

❑ Construct a pyramid, page 72.

❑ Make and use a solar cooker, page 63.

Lesson 5

❑ Continue Vocabulary Activities, page 25.

❑ Complete animal research and make animal mobiles, pages 30–32.

❑ Decorate a bulletin board. (See page 77.)

❑ Learn about Aztec food and complete the activities on pages 66-67.

❑ Add any new information to the Cultural Time Line, page 60.

Lesson 6

❑ Enjoy a cup of hot chocolate, page 67.

❑ Be an Aztec city-planner. Make a map of your city and write a brochure explaining its benefits to a tourist or newcomer.

❑ Research life in modern Mexico City. Describe the city from the point of view of an Aztec warrior.

❑ Pass out the lists of questions that students wrote before they started the unit on the Aztecs. Have them add the answers that they know. Use the unanswered questions to compile an end-of-the-unit quiz.

Overview of Activities

Setting the Stage

1. Prepare a bulletin board to look like a landscape. (See page 77.)

2. Have each student fold a piece of lined paper in half vertically. On one side, have the students write any information, words, phrases, etc., that they already know about the Aztecs. On the other half, have them write any questions they have about the Aztecs. Share the questions with the class so that the students can add to their lists. Save the papers until the end of the section on Aztecs. The classroom goal is to answer as many of the questions as possible by the end of the unit. The teacher should record the students' questions to use as a guideline in selecting activities and to make an end-of-the-unit quiz.

3. Add books, magazines, maps, pictures, etc., about the Aztecs, pyramids, calendars, mosaics, jaguars, the sun and the moon, and Mexico to the research area. Ask the students to bring in items from home, like postcards, stamps, magazine pictures, mosaic samples, coins, etc. to share, or add to the display.

4. Listen to some music from Mexico. A good source is *Fiesta Musical* from Warner Bros. Records.

5. Read some factual and contemporary literature and legends about the Aztecs.

Factual:	*The Aztecs* by Donna Walsh Shepherd (Franklin Watts, 1992)
Contemporary:	"Paleton and the Musical Elephant" by Jorge Ibarguengoitia in *Where Angels Glide at Dawn* (Econo-Clad, 1999)
Legend:	*Opposum and the Great Firemaker: A Mexican Legend* by Jan M. Mike (Troll Associates, 1993)

Enjoying the Book

1. Create a time line showing these years: 1428, 1492, 1502, 1519, 1521, 1524, and 1822. Add information from the book to the chart as you read. Study the time line on pages 47 and 48 of the book to understand 25 centuries of civilization in the Americas.

2. Study the diagram of Aztec society on pages 34-35 of the book. Choose one category of people and write a brief report explaining the activities of their typical day. As a class, make a chart comparing the lifestyles of the Aztec people. Consider these categories: homes, belongings, jobs, entertainment, food, clothing, and interesting facts.

3. Use the information you have learned from the book to discuss the following questions:

   • Why do you believe the Aztec people chose to settle in this region?

   • How do archaeologists know that the Aztecs had a strong central government?

   • What are some technical advances of this society in architecture and city planning?

Overview of Activities *(cont.)*

Enjoying the Book *(cont.)*

4. The sun was extremely important to the Aztecs, who called themselves "People of the Sun." Read about the sun, pages 61–62. Have students create Aztec sun god masks, page 61.

5. Powerful Aztec knights were called jaguar knights and wore the skin of the jaguar when they went into batttle. Students can research other animals native to Mexico and Central America and use the information to make a mobile, page 32.

6. Find the picture of Quetzalcoatl, "the feathered serpent," on page 43. Of what was he the god? What is a serpent? Have the students draw a picture of what the god of nature might have looked like in human form. Find the legend of Quetzalcoatl in a reference book.

Extending the Book

1. Use reference books and reread each section of this book to create charts showing details of the physical and cultural environment in Aztec society. Here are some ideas for categories: animals (wild and domesticated), geography and climate, food, plants and trees, religion, education, art and music, military, government, and clothing. Make notes and list the sources (including page numbers) where you find the information.

2. Imagine you are an Aztec city-planner. How would you choose a location? Draw a map of your city showing homes for all classes of people, city walls/gates, temple/pyramids, roads, farms/gardens, and the Emperor's palace.

3. Describe life in your city to a person who is deciding to visit or live there. Explain what goes on each day and why it is a good or bad place to live or visit.

4. Mexico City is built over the site of the Aztec Great Pyramid. Research what remains of the ancient city. Suppose you were a young Aztec warrior who magically returned to the modern city. What would you see? Smell? Hear?

5. Pass out the lists students wrote before they started the unit on Aztecs. Have them answer any of their questions or add new information they learned. Have the students write questions for a quiz. Compile their questions for an end-of-the-unit quiz.

6. If the Spanish conquistadors had not taken chocolate back to Europe, the chocolate bar might never have been invented. Have a classroom chocolate festival. Have the students bring in their favorite foods and recipes that include chocolate. (Teacher Note: Offer an alternate treat for students who can not have chocolate.)

Vocabulary Activities

• pyramid	• serpent	• ceremonies	• sacred
• jaguar	• rubble	• dwellers	• loom
• empire	• sacrifice	• calendars	• civilization
• fortress	• siege	• causeway	• aqueducts
• aviaries	• idol	• gape	• attire
• tribute	• expedition	• foe	• codex
• tactics	• ritual	• omen	• glyphs

1. Categories

Arrange words in groups according to parts of speech (nouns, verbs, adjectives, etc.) or by the number of syllables in each word.

2. Bingo

Assign each student a word to define. Have each student write the word and definition on a strip of paper. Give students blank Bingo cards, and instruct them to write "free" in the center box and add words of their choice to the remaining boxes. The caller reads only the definitions. Since the Aztecs loved chocolate, give miniature chocolate bars as prizes.

3. Picture Dictionary

Write each word on a piece of paper. The students randomly choose a paper. Have each student draw a picture (no words allowed!) to represent that word. Put all their pictures on the chalkboard, or wall. Have the class discuss which words match which pictures. Add words to the pictures and put them together as a class book.

4. Word lines

Write each word on a small piece of paper. Use clothespins to clip the words in alphabetical order to a piece of string stretched across the room. Add new words to the wordline as you read more information about the Aztecs.

5. Let Them Teach

Let the students take over the teaching. Divide them into working groups to design a worksheet using as many of the words as they can. Make classroom copies, and then each day as you begin the unit, pass out a new puzzle to complete. The group who designed each worksheet is also in charge of giving directions, monitoring the room and answering questions, and grading the finished work.

The Aztecs' Journey

The Aztecs were the last people to settle in the Valley of Mexico, high in the volcanic mountains of central Mexico. There, on the shores of shallow, marshy Lake Tezcoco, they built an impressive center for their empire.

The Aztecs were a semi-nomadic tribe of Chichimecs who arrived in the Valley of Mexico about A.D. 1200. According to oral traditions and codices, the ancestral home of the Aztecs was Aztlan, a place northwest of Mexico City. No one has identified an exact location. About A.D. 1100 the god *Huizilopochtli* (Blue Hummingbird) instructed them to wander until they found an eagle on a cactus, eating a snake. Here they would build their capital.

After many stops and skirmishes, they settled on the west side of Tetzcoco, at a place called *Chapultapec* (Grasshopper Hill). Other tribes drove the Aztecs out, but the Colhua allowed the Aztecs to live near them in exchange for the services of Aztec soldiers. Finally tired of being under Colhuacans, Aztecs killed the daughter of the ruler, then fled into the marshy lake. On one island, they saw an eagle on a cactus. At the site of this sign, the Aztecs built their capital, Tenochtitlán.

In the 200 years from the sighting of the eagle (about A.D. 1325) to the arrival of the Spanish (A.D. 1521), the Aztecs grew to be the most powerful people in the Valley of Mexico. They adopted many elements from the cultures that had preceded them and built one of the most impressive cities of Mesoamerica.

Use colored pencils, maps, atlases, and resource books to complete the map activities on page 27.

Critical Thinking

1. What is the ancient city of Tenochtitlán called today?
2. What state would the ancient city of Monte Alban be located in today?
3. Draw a "then and now" map about a different subject:
    a. the state you live in
    b. Native American tribes
    c. the ancient Egyptians
    d. the Roman Empire
    e. your hometown—100 years ago and now

4. What modern symbol has on it an eagle on a cactus, eating a snake?

Map Activities

Aztecs: The Fall of the Aztec Capital

Use a reference book or the Internet for help in completing this page.

What source did you use? _____

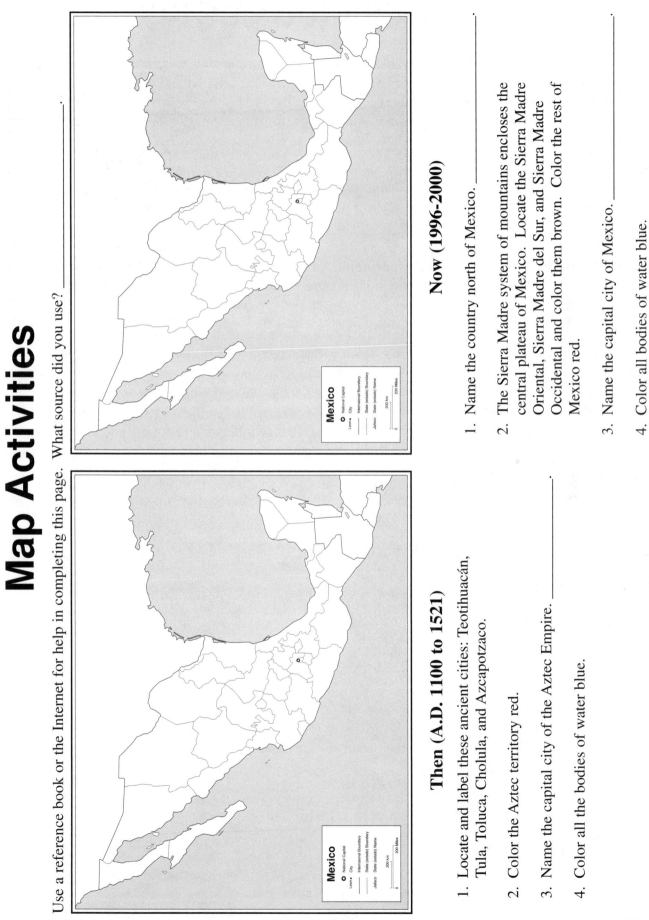

Now (1996-2000)

1. Name the country north of Mexico. _____

2. The Sierra Madre system of mountains encloses the central plateau of Mexico. Locate the Sierra Madre Oriental, Sierra Madre del Sur, and Sierra Madre Occidental and color them brown. Color the rest of Mexico red.

3. Name the capital city of Mexico. _____

4. Color all bodies of water blue.

Then (A.D. 1100 to 1521)

1. Locate and label these ancient cities: Teotihuacán, Tula, Toluca, Cholula, and Azcapotzaco.

2. Color the Aztec territory red.

3. Name the capital city of the Aztec Empire. _____

4. Color all the bodies of water blue.

Aztec Codices

The Aztecs used a written language that consisted of pictures representing spoken words and phrases. A drawing of a footprint meant travel, while a scroll meant speech. Individual pictures, called glyphs, were combined to show compound words or tell a story. The symbol for the city of Tenochtitlán, which means cactus stone, uses the glyph for cactus with a glyph for stone.

Manuscripts called *codices* (singular: *codex*) recorded the Aztec story and detailed religious ceremonies, calendars, speeches, tax information, and even how to bring up children. When the Spanish took control of the Aztec Empire, they could not understand the glyphs and thought they were magic and evil. So the Spanish bishops pledged to wipe out "the heresy of the New World," and most of the Aztec codices were burned. Fortunately, later missionaries felt that they needed to understand Aztec practices and habits in order to eradicate them and set about gathering and recording as much information as possible. They learned *Nahuatl*, the Aztec language, and hired scribes to record interviews with Aztec informants. Several codices were re-created from the rich Aztec oral tradition and Spanish translations were added. The missionaries also created dictionaries and glossaries of the Nahuatl language, using their own Spanish alphabet to record the sounds of the oral Aztec language.

A codex consisted of glyphs printed on leather or paper made from the inside of a wild fig tree's bark. To make the paper, the bark fibers were stripped off, soaked in lime water, and then pounded into sheets with stones. After it dried, the paper was coated with starch to make it white. Ink made from a thick resin of animal and vegetable dyes was used so that it would not run on the very soft paper. The color and size of glyphs were important. Important people were drawn larger, and color (bright red, yellow, blue, and green) was added to show rank. When the record was complete, the paper was folded like an accordion, and a cover was added.

Make a Codex

Materials: a long, narrow strip of white paper; paint or markers; cardboard

Directions: Fold the paper like an accordion to make panels.

Choose or create a story to tell. Use Aztec glyphs or make your own glyphs to tell your story. You may add some labels in English, as the Spanish did, to help the reader understand what the pictures mean.

Share your story aloud.

Extensions:

Use a long, narrow piece of white butcher paper and make one large classroom codex telling the story of *Aztecs: The Fall of the Aztec Capital (DK Discoveries)*, or a Mexican legend.

Research methods of making paper. Demonstrate one for the class or use it to make your codex.

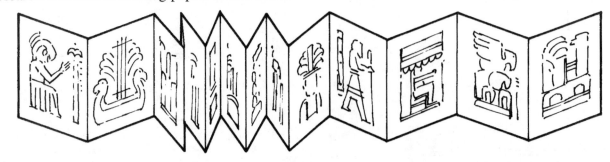

Aztec Calendar Stone

In 1790, workers in Mexico City unearthed relics of the Aztec religion. The first was a statue that was 8 feet, 5 inches (2.5 m) long. The Spanish viceroy of Mexico City became interested in this find and ordered that it be taken to the university for study. By doing this, he reversed the policy of the conquistadors and their descendants who, for almost three centuries, had destroyed all signs of the conquered Indians.

The next major discovery was a carved stone 4 feet (1.2 m) thick and 12 feet (3.7 m) in diameter which weighed 24 tons (21.7 metric tons). Covered with carved geometric symbols, the center features a human-like face with a knife blade for the tongue. This piece became known as the *Stone of the Sun*, because it resembles a sundial. It has also been called the *Aztec Calendar Stone* because the outer carvings are the Aztec glyphs for the 20-day calendar. Archaeologists have determined that this piece expresses the Aztecs' belief that there had been four suns (ages) and that they were living in the fifth sun. This fifth sun is represented by the face of *Tonatiuh* (the sun in the sky) in the stone's center. He is surrounded by symbols of the destruction (*by jaguars, winds [hurricanes], fires [volcanoes], and rains*) of the four previous worlds. The stone also foretells the end of the fifth sun on the date *"4 Movement."*

Make a Sun God Mosaic

Materials: pictures of the Aztec calendar (See page 45, *Aztecs: The Fall of the Aztec Capital.*); tagboard, old file folders, or paper plates; variety of paper scraps (construction paper or magazine pages); glue and scissors

Directions:

1. Cut a large circle from the tagboard.
2. Draw a simple design on the tagboard. Start in the middle with a picture of a sun god and then continue to create patterns in rings around the center.
3. Cut your paper scraps into different square and rectangular shapes. Keep your colors in separate stacks.
4. Glue individual squares within your pencil design until you have completed the circle.
5. Variations: Use different types of mosiac materials such as dyed eggshells, seeds and beans, macaroni, material scraps, and foils.

Critical Thinking

The Maya and Aztecs knew and used the discus shape for their calendars. Why did they not apply it in their everyday life as a wheel?

The Emperor's Zoo

Moctezuma had aviaries, ponds, and a zoo on the palace grounds. He enjoyed strolling through his gardens and was entertained by the exotic birds and animals. Hundreds of servants were employed to care for the animals.

Animal	the jaguar, in Spanish "el tigre"
Classification	mammal
Size	from five to eight feet (1.5 to 2.4 m) in length, and weighs 100 to 250 pounds (45 to 113 kg)
Habitat	low coastal forests, ranges from Mexico down the coast to Argentina, one of the best tree climbers of the big cats (a favorite hangout is dangling on limbs of trees), expert swimmer quick and agile
Food Source	deer, capybaras, tapirs, peccaries, other small mammals, has been seen catching fish to eat, stalks its prey or ambushes it from a hiding spot
Appearance	a short, stiff coat, golden or buff in color with black rosettes, sometimes with dark brown or black coats
Environment Concerns	The jaguar has been relentlessly hunted for its valuable coat, and by farmers, who see it as a livestock killer. The forest habitat is being sheared and put to ranching and farm use, affecting the hunting grounds of the jaguar.

There are many different animals living in Mexico and Central America today. Research one, using the information you find to complete the chart on page 31. Then turn your information into a mobile on page 32.

- flamingo
- crocodile
- macaw
- tapir
- vampire bat
- ocelot

- anteater
- howler monkey
- spider monkey
- iguana
- armadillo
- boa constrictor

- vulture
- tiger
- coyote
- chameleons
- toucan
- hummingbird

- tree frogs
- butterfly
- anaconda
- parrot
- lynx
- wolves

Animal Information

Animal	Classification	Size	Habitat	Food Source	Appearance	Environment Concerns

Animal Mobiles

Materials: copies of pattern on white construction paper, needle, 12 inches (30 cm) thread, ¼ plastic straw, paper clip, scissors, thimble

Directions:

1. Cut the piece of straw into three pieces. Cut out the ring shapes following the dotted lines and discard the extra pieces, leaving one solid circle and three paper rings.

2. Draw a picture of your animal on one side of the solid center piece. Write the animal's name on the back. Write the rest of your animal information on the other rings, in any order you wish. Use both sides and add color and designs to fill in empty spaces.

3. Thread the needle and make a large knot in the end of the thread. Poke a hole with the needle in the top of the solid center piece. Tie the thread to the center piece, then push the needle sideways through a piece of straw. (Be careful not to poke your finger). Next, thread the needle through the next circle, like taking a stitch. Add another piece of straw. Continue alternating circles and straw pieces. Hold it up to check how it looks.

4. Remove the needle and tie the thread to a paper clip to make a hanging hook. Display the mobile in the classroom.

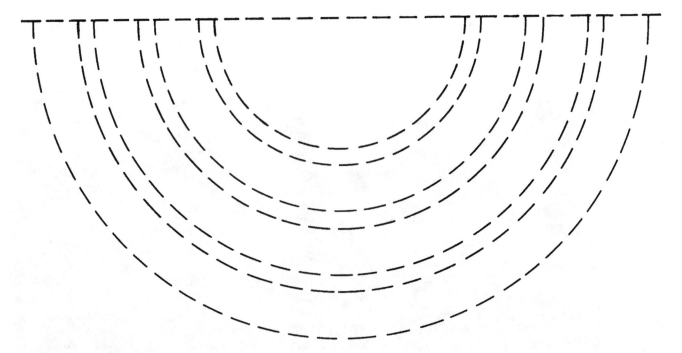

Aztec Who's Who

These short biographies are about three people who played important roles in the fall of the Aztec Empire.

Hernando Cortés

On his last voyage in 1502, Columbus claimed Central and South America for the Spanish crown. Many Europeans came to the New World as settlers, explorers, and conquistadors. One of them was Hernando Cortés.

Cortés left his native Spain in 1504 to seek fame and fortune in the New World. After seven years as a planter in Hispaniola (now known as Haiti) and a term as a soldier on the island of Cuba, Cortés sailed west in 1519 with 600 armed soldiers and 16 horses and landed on the Mexican coast. The Aztec ruler, Moctezuma, thought Cortés was a god and sent envoys with gifts. This only increased Cortés' desire for gold.

Cortés won easy victories as he moved closer and closer to the Aztec capital city, Tenochtitlán. Moctezuma feared these bearded strangers and allowed them to enter the city. Cortés was treated as a god with gifts and privileges. He soon tricked Moctezuma, took him hostage, and ruled the city.

Meanwhile, Spanish forces had arrived on the coast to arrest Cortés for disobedience because he did not have permission to make the expedition. While Cortés was defending himself on the coast, his officers attacked and killed many unarmed Aztecs during a sacred ceremony. The people revolted. Cortés returned and attempted to calm the revolt. Instead, Moctezuma was killed, and Cortés fled the city with his soldiers.

A year later, Cortés returned with a new army of Spanish soldiers and Aztec enemies and laid siege to Tenochtitlán. After 75 days, the city fell. Cortés now controlled the Aztec Empire. He ordered his soldiers to raze the city. The gold and treasures of the Aztecs were sent back to Spain. Cortés returned to Spain in 1539, where he died in 1547.

Moctezuma II

Emperor Moctezuma II, also known as Montezuma, whose name means "Angry Lord," became the ruler of the Aztecs in 1502, when the empire was at its height. He was responsible for the construction of many temples, hospitals, and aqueducts. In 1519, the last year of the 52-year cycle on the Aztec calendar, catastrophes plagued the land, convincing Moctezuma that he was destined to see the Aztec world end. Adding to his fear, it was the year *1 Reed* on the Aztec calendar. A legend predicted that the god Quetzalcoatl would return from exile that year, reclaim his throne, and destroy the Aztec Empire. At first, Moctezuma believed Cortés was that feared god.

Aztec Who's Who (cont.)

Moctezuma II (cont.)

When special rituals and ceremonies failed to make the Spanish leave, Moctezuma offered them gifts and invited them into the capital city of Tenochtitlán. It was a mistake. Cortés took Moctezuma hostage and ruled the empire through him. When the Aztecs revolted after an attack by Spanish soldiers, Moctezuma attempted to calm the citizens of Tenochtitlán. However, they refused to listen to his pleas for an end to the battles, believing that Moctezuma was on the side of the Spanish. Moctezuma was pelted with stones and died. (One source claims that the leader was actually stabbed by the Spaniards.) Cortés, fearing for his life, fled with his soldiers. Cortés returned with more Spanish soldiers and other tribes who hated the Aztecs. Within two years, in 1521, the Aztec Empire fell.

Doña Marina

An Aztec girl, sold as a slave to the Maya, helped Cortés in his conquest of the Aztecs. The girl, named Marina by Cortés, spoke the Aztec language, Nahuatl, and one of the Mayan languages. Working with a shipwrecked Spaniard, Jeronimo de Aguilar, who had learned Mayan, Cortés used a three-step communication process to learn about the Aztecs from Marina.

Doña Marina counseled Cortés on the ways of the Aztecs and became invaluable as a spy. She informed Cortés about many surprise attacks and secret plots. Moctezuma tried repeatedly to capture Cortés, but each time Doña Marina warned Cortés. After two years of battles, the Spanish controlled the Aztec Empire and their gold. But with all her importance to Cortés, nothing is known about what happened to Doña Marina after the fall of the Aztec Empire. What do you think happened to her?

Activities

1. Imagine that you are one of these three historic characters and that you were in Tenochtitlán during the Aztec revolt. Write a paragraph describing the event from the perspective of your character.

2. Make a three-way Venn diagram to compare and contrast the facts from these three points of view.

3. In small groups, create a short play involving the three characters. For example: Moctezuma plots to kill Cortés, but Doña Marina spies and foils the attack. Perform your play for the class.

Secret of the Andes

by Ann Nolan Clark

Summary

This Newbery Award Book tells the story of a young Inca boy and his llama. Through his adventures, Cusi learns the secret of his birth and his ancient ancestors. Can he prove himself worthy of this secret? Will he accept his place in the ancient order? The book describes the rituals of the ancient Inca civilization and the beauty of the Andes mountains and valleys.

The outline shown below is a suggested plan for using the various activities that are presented in this unit. You should adapt these ideas to fit your classroom situation.

Sample Lesson Plan

Lesson 1
- ❏ Introduce *Secret of the Andes.*
- ❏ Choose one or more activities from Setting the Stage, page 36.
- ❏ Play a video about the Inca Empire.
- ❏ Make tissue paper banners to decorate the room. (page 78)

Lesson 2
- ❏ Read chapters, 1, 2, and 3.
- ❏ Choose an item from Enjoying the Book, pages 36–37, to complete as you read each chapter.
- ❏ Discuss questions and choose items from Chapter Activities, page 38.
- ❏ Read about the Inca Empire, and complete the activity, pages 44–45.

Lesson 3
- ❏ Read Chapters 4, 5, and 6.
- ❏ Discuss questions and choose items from Chapter Activities, page 39.
- ❏ Practice weaving with paper, page 48.
- ❏ Add Inca information to the Cultural Time Line, page 60.
- ❏ Learn about Inca food, pages 68–69.
- ❏ Begin Myths, Legends, and Fables project, pages 52–53.

Lesson 4
- ❏ Read Chapters 7, 8, and 9.
- ❏ Discuss questions and choose items from Chapter Activities, page 40.
- ❏ Complete the The Lost City of Machu Picchu activity, page 47.
- ❏ Begin a yarn weaving project, page 49.

Lesson 5
- ❏ Read Chapters 10, 11, and 12.
- ❏ Discuss questions and choose items from Chapter Activities, page 41.
- ❏ Complete the The Llama, page 50.
- ❏ Complete the Inca Word Problems on page 51.
- ❏ Finish yarn weaving.
- ❏ Continue myths, legends, and fables.

Lesson 6
- ❏ Read Chapters 13, 14, and 15.
- ❏ Discuss questions and choose items from Chapter Activities, pages 41–42.
- ❏ Make a mola, page 71.

Lesson 7
- ❏ Read Chapters 16 and 17.
- ❏ Discuss questions and choose items from Chapter Activities, page 42
- ❏ Do the crossword puzzle, page 43.
- ❏ Complete the Double Talk, activity page 46.
- ❏ Continue myths, legends, and fables.

Lesson 8
- ❏ Choose one or more activities from Extending the Book page 37.
- ❏ Complete the Rewriting History activities, page 54.
- ❏ Begin work on culminating activities, pages 74–76.
- ❏ Add details to the Inca bulletin board.

Overview of Activities

Setting the Stage

1. Prepare a bulletin board to look like the Andes Mountains landscape. (See page 77.)

2. Have students locate Peru on a world map. Discuss its location in relation to the Mayan and Aztec Empires. Complete the student map activities on pages 44 and 45.

3. Next, introduce *Secret of the Andes* by showing students the cover, illustrations, and reading the back cover and introduction.

4. Prepare a research and work area in the classroom with information, books, maps etc. about Incas, the Andes Mountains, weaving, and llamas. Have students bring in items like postcards, stamps, magazines, pictures, ponchos, coins, etc., to share or display.

5. Show *The Inca: Secrets of the Ancestors* from Time-Life's *Lost Civilizations* series or another video about the Inca Empire.

6. Potatoes were an important staple to the Inca. Ask each student to bring in a potato and a wide mouth jar. Insert four toothpicks evenly into one end of the potato and suspend the potato from the jar rim. Fill the jar with water. While you read the book, record, measure, and graph the growth of the potatoes. Change the water about once a week.

Enjoying the Book

1. Assign a number of pages for reading each day. See the Sample Lesson Plan, page 35, for suggestions. The Chapter Activities, pages 38–42, provide discussion questions and activities to guide the reading process.

2. Cover a can or box. Make name strips from old file folders, one for each student reading the book. Place the name strips in the can. At the end of each chapter, choose three names. Give each of these students a piece of colored paper cut in any shape and ask them to write the following on the paper

   a. an interesting word and its definition from the reading pages
   b. the name of the chapter and what it represents or means
   c. the most important event that happened in the chapter

   Add these papers to the Andes Mountains bulletin board in a random pattern as you complete each chapter.

Overview of Activities *(cont.)*

Enjoying the Book *(cont.)*

3. Create a Vocabulary Dictionary as you read each chapter. This can be done as a class on large sheets of butcher paper, on an overhead transparency, or in individual books. Suggested vocabulary words for each chapter are included in the Chapter Activities, pages 38–42.

4. Use the vocabulary words from each chapter and play a word game, like hangman, or bingo.

5. Continue adding to the time line. Compare the development of the Inca to the cultures of Central America.

6. A variety of Peruvian artifacts, crafts, and informational materials, including musical instruments and cassettes of traditional music, are available from Ethnic Arts & Facts, (510) 465-0451.

Extending the Book

1. Read books and stories about the Incas that are factual, contemporary and legends.

   Factual: *The Incas* by Shirlee P. Newman (Franklin Watts)
   Contemporary: "Tarma" by Maria Fort from *Where Angels Glide At Dawn,* (Harper Trophy)
   Legend: *The Llama's Secret* by Argentina Palacios (Troll Associates)

2. There are many poems, chants, and songs in the book. Make enlarged copies of them. Have each student choose a selection to present orally to the class. Play instrumental music and recite poetry for an afternoon.

3. The Nazca, an earlier people of Peru, carved a network of lines in the highlands, which is only visible from the air. No one knows what these lines represent or how they were created. One writer theorized that they were runways for spaceships and that visitors from outer space were instrumental in the development of advanced cultures in the Americas. Discuss this theory with the students. Ask them to decide whether or not they believe in the UFO theory and to write paragraphs defending their positions. As an alternative, use this theory as the basis of a creative story.

4. Have a potato fest. Have the students bring in their favorite potato treats or recipes. Ask students to illustrate their recipes; then, make a potato cookbook. Duplicate pages and give a copy to each student or create an entire menu of food made from potatoes in different shapes and forms.

Chapter Activities

Chapter 1—"Hidden Valley"

For Discussion: a. What does Cusi see in the valley below? Why does this excite him? b. What animals do the old man, Chuto, and the young boy, Cusi, raise? c. What is a minstrel and what type of instrument does he play? d. Why is Cusi excited about going on a journey?

Activity: Begin a character chart. As new characters are introduced, record adjectives used to describe them, and list interesting sayings or quotations, important actions, etc.

Vocabulary: peak, sheer, mantles, minstrel, poncho, shin, corral, gourds

Chapter 2—"Sunrise Call"

For Discussion: a. What sound do llamas make? b. What does Chuto do each morning? Why is this morning special?

Activity: Make panpipes, which the Inca call *zampoñia*. The Inca used bones or bamboo to make their pipes, but you can make them with plastic drinking straws, hollow bamboo canes (from a garden store), or plastic or metal tubing. Cut the straws or tubing into pieces of different lengths. Start with one inch (2.5 cm) and make each piece one inch (2.5 cm) longer. Cut two wedged-shaped pieces of corrugated paper and arrange the straws on one wedge so that the tops are level. Glue the second wedge over the straws, making a "sandwich." Add strips of cardboard to the top and bottom edges for strength. Decorate with paint. To play your pipes, keep your head still and move the pipes as you blow.

Vocabulary: lest, stunted, sentinels, boulders, gnarled, fleet, somber

Chapter 3—"Llama-Humming"

For Discussion: a. What do llamas do when they are displeased? b. How does the author describe the sound of llamas humming? c. What does the minstrel tell Cusi about black llamas?

Activities: 1. Make a list of the traits mentioned about llamas. Compare it to a list of traits about a pet or favorite animal. Do research to learn more about llamas, vicunas, guanacos, and alpacas. 2. Read the Greek myth about Pan aloud to the class. Compare Pan and the minstrel.

Vocabulary: herd, matted, pulp, strands, staff, bounding

Chapter Activities *(cont.)*

Chapter 4—"Singer of Songs"

For Discussion: a. Why is Cusi so interested in the family below the valley? b. What is *chuno*? How is it prepared? c. How does the minstrel describe the ancient city of Cuzco? What does Cusi imagine when he hears this chant? d. Why is Cusi troubled by the minstrel's last song?

Activity: Potatoes are a very nutritious food. Research the nutritional value of potatoes. Brainstorm a list of favorite ways to eat potatoes. Use the list to plan one or more days of potato meals.

Vocabulary: mortar, thongs, pestle, fringed, droned, gruel, fiesta, wailing, vaguely

Chapter 5—"The Steep Trail"

For Discussion: a. How does the minstrel describe Hidden Valley and the world outside? How does Chuto answer? b. What gift does the minstrel give Chuto for the journey? c. What items do Chuto and Cusi take with them on their journey to the Salt Pits? d. Describe Cusi's feelings about crossing the swinging bridges and climbing the tree ladder.

Activity: Divide the class into small groups and challenge each group to construct a rope bridge from one desk or chair to another, using scraps of yarn and string. Have the class devise a way to measure which bridge can support the most weight.

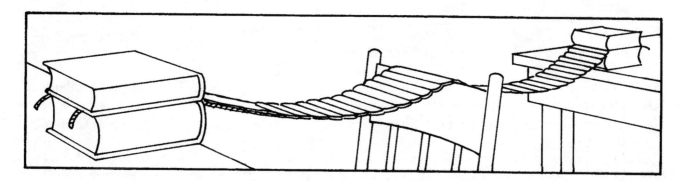

Vocabulary: heralding, ford, sash, loomed, plaited, hinder, chasm, wisps, pillar, vivid

Chapter 6—"The Long Way"

For Discussion: a. How does the change in altitude affect Cusi? b. Why is the small village called Condor Kuncca?

Activity: Make a list of the plants and animal tracks Chuto shows to Cusi in the jungle.

Vocabulary: streamlet, seeped, threshing, dense, bleak, terraces, crest

Chapter 7—"Questions"

For Discussion: a. What differences does Cusi notice between the Spanish people of the hacienda and the Indians? b. Explain how the people of the village tilled the soil without a plow. c. At one point Chuto says "The llamas remember." What is he trying to explain?

Chapter Activities *(cont.)*

Chapter 7—"Questions" *(cont.)*

Activity: Create a color wheel of words and descriptions used in the book. Draw a large circle. Every time you find a color mentioned, write the word and what it is describing in a section of the circle. Color in that section the appropriate color.

Vocabulary: frail, *hacienda*, indignant, *burros*, spade, vast, basin, *pampas*

Chapter 8—"Outside"

For Discussion: a. Explain how salt is collected. Why do you think salt is important? b. Why do Chuto and Cusi chew coca leaves as they work?

Activity: Cusi is amazed when he sees a truck for the first time. Choose another invention, like a telephone or television, and describe what it would look, sound, and smell like from Cusi's viewpoint.

Vocabulary: brine, glaring, barter, dusk, clamor, frugally, granite, precious

Chapter 9—"Amauta Comes"

For Discussion: a. Explain the importance of llamas to Cusi's existence. b. Why is a silver llama special? c. What does Amauta have in common with Cusi?

Activity: Cusi uses a "string of thinking" to remember events in sequence. Think about an important trip, period of time in your life, or a favorite story. Number a piece of paper from one to eight and write one word as a knot on each line. Share your story to the class, using your word knots to help you remember details and order.

Vocabulary: iridescent, shearing, whet, fleece, quench, rouse, coaxed, cringe

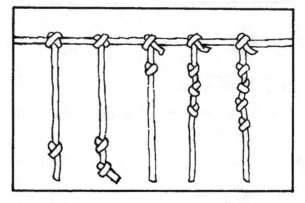

Chapter 10—"A Mission Unshared"

For Discussion: a. What things does Cusi learn from the Amauta? b. What do the colors of the quipu cord represent? c. How many llamas are chosen? Describe the characteristics that Cusi looks for when choosing the llamas.

Chapter Activities *(cont.)*

Chapter 10—"A Mission Unshared" *(cont.)*

Activity: The Incas kept detailed records using *quipus*. To make a *quipu*, cut string or yarn into pieces 30 inches (76 cm) long. Give each student six pieces. Attach five of the pieces to the sixth by tying a knot. The Inca used a decimal system like our number system. Tell students that units (1–9) will be tied at the bottom of the cord. Tens will begin at the 10-inch (25 cm) mark and hundreds at the 20-inch (50 cm) mark. On the first cord, tie knots to represent the number of girls in the class; on the second, represent the number of boys. On the third and fourth cords, show the number of boys and girls in the whole school. On the fifth, record the number of pets owned by the students or other information. Have students make up a report using their *quipu* facts. (If desired, white string can be colored with markers to enhance memory, i.e., blue for boys, red for girls.)

Vocabulary: deeds, lore, *maize*, rites, quivered, squint, kindled, mission

Chapter 11—"The Sign"

For Discussion: a. Where does Misti lead Cusi? b. What sign does Cusi find, and what does it mean? c. What does Cusi hope to find on his journey? Do you think he will be successful?

Activity: Draw a picture of what you think the white marble *dais* and golden sandals look like when Cusi finds them.

Vocabulary: thicket, meandered, hand-hewn, massive, awe, dais, anew

Chapter 12—"The Valley Below"

For Discussion: a. Who is Misti, and how does he help Cusi? b. What does Cusi feel like when he crosses the clearing and finds the family has gone? c. What does he decide to do next?

Activity: Make a list of what Cusi packs for his journey. Imagine yourself on a similar trip. Decide where you will go and how long it will take. Draw a picture of yourself and eight llamas. Identify what is in each pack and why you would need it on your trip.

Vocabulary: bobbed, procession, *vicuña*, marred, eternal, thatch, *siesta*, haven

Chapter 13—"Cuzco Trail"

For Discussion: a. How does Cusi decide which way to go at the fork in the road? b. Describe the old man and woman that Cusi meets. Who do you think they were?

Activity: Use a large piece of white paper folded in half. On one half, draw what the town of Cuzco might have looked like from the hilltop. On the other half, draw a picture of your school or neighborhood and what it looks like from the top of a hill. Add color and labels.

Vocabulary: haze, majestic, *Ayllu*, rasp, *pueblo*, sacred, *vague*

Chapter Activities *(cont.)*

Chapter 14—"The Marketplace"

For Discussion: a. Explain ways that the city of Cuzco is different from Cuzi's highland valley home. b. What is bartering? c. What items does Cusi barter for his wool?

Activity: Ask students to bring in items (paperback books, baked goods, pencils, trading cards, candy) to trade. At a designated time, everyone displays his/her goods and trading begins. Remind the students that the Inca used *yapa* (something extra) to show good faith.

Vocabulary: homage, intricate, fragile, beckoned, sedate, loiter, scarlet, pealing

Chapter 15—"The Family"

For Discussion: a. Does Cusi find a family? b. What are they like? c. Does Cusi stay with the family? Why or why not?

Activity: Create a family tree for the family Cusi meets. Make your own family tree. Compare and share them with the other students in the class.

Vocabulary: *mantilla,* keen, omen, *centavo,* grieve, smoldering

Chapter 16—"Keeper of the Fields"

For Discussion: a. How do the golden sandals help Cusi make his decision? b. Explain the saying "Grieve not if your searching circles." How does this relate to Cusi?

Activity: Paint or color a picture of a sunrise. When it dries, using a calligraphy pen, copy the "Sunrise Call" across the picture. Or create your own "Sunrise Call" poem to print across the picture.

Vocabulary: gesture, gaze, rivulet, babbled, thaw, haughty, lurked

Chapter 17—"Written in the Stars"

For Discussion: a. What is the Secret of the Andes? b. What vow does Cusi make?

Activity: Read the poems and vows in this chapter as a choral reading. Divide the class into small groups. Each group decides how to divide the poems, practices reading, and then presents their reading to the class.

Vocabulary: wistful, falter, diluted, vow, novice, pivoted, wrath, herald

Vocabulary Crossword

Complete the crossword puzzle, using vocabulary words.

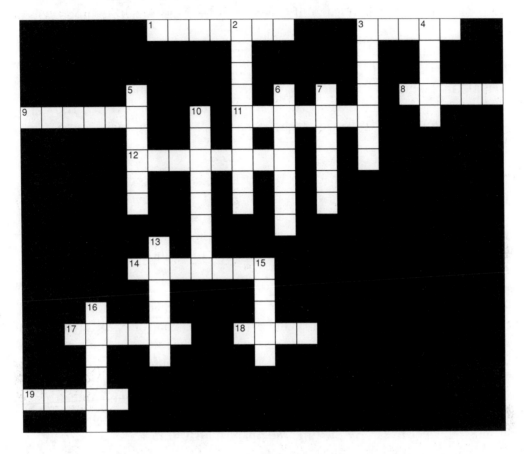

Across

1. braided
3. stick used to aid in walking; a sign of authority
8. perceived as bright and distinct; brilliant
9. blanket-like cloak with a hole in the center for the head
11. vivid red color
12. bouncing; echoing
14. making a long, loud, high-pitched cry
17. persuaded, or tried to persuade, by flattery
18. sharply pointed mountain top
19. gloomy or dreary

Down

2. to beat the stems and husks of plants to separate straw from grains
3. prevented from growing; dwarfed
4. physically weak; not strong or substantial
5. dark, gloomy; serious
6. scornful and condescendingly proud
7. coat of wool from a sheep or other animal
10. wandering musician and/or poet
13. to trade goods or services without money
15. a thin watery porridge
16. an enclosure for confining livestock

Make three columns on the back of this paper. Label them noun, verb, and adjective. Write the words from the puzzle in the right column. Some words have more than one use. If you are not sure how the word is being used, find the original sentence in the book.

The Inca Empire

Archaeologists have identified several groups of people who settled in ancient Peru. Along the coast the Nazca and Mochica tribes flourished from A.D. 200 to 600. In the highlands, near Lake Titicaca, Tiahuanaco and Huari people built roads, towns and temples. These empires collapsed about A.D. 1000. Then, about A.D. 1200, the first Inca, Manco Capac, arrived at the Cuzco Valley.

No one is sure if Manco Capac was real or legendary. According to the traditional stories, he was the son of the Sun God, sent to earth to found a people with his sisters and brothers. They settled in the Cuzco Valley where they built a small, strong state, *Tahuantinsuyu* (The Land of the Four Quarters), ruled by the descendants of Manco Capac, who were called *Inca* (lord or king).

Then, in 1438, the neighboring Chancas threatened to invade Cuzco. The Inca, Pachacuti, lead his army to victory and expanded his control of the area. He is also credited with rebuilding the city of Cuzco. Archaeologists think this city was planned to look like a puma. Pachacuti was Inca until his death in 1471.

The rulers who followed Pachacuti were called *Sapa Inca,* and continued expanding the Inca Empire, sometimes through wars and sometimes by promising better lives. By the time the Spanish arrived in 1532, the Tahuantinsuyu people and their Inca leaders controlled the west coast of South America from Quito in the north to what is now Chile in the south, a distance of 2,170 miles (3,500 km). The empire included diverse terrain, from the Andes mountains to deserts and coastal areas. The Incas imposed their religion, laws, and Quechua language on those they conquered, and they collected taxes from the people. A vast system of roads connected all parts of the Inca lands to the capital at Cuzco, carrying armies, officials, and goods. Messengers, called *chasquis,* used the roads to carry communications between Cuzco and its regional capitals.

At its height, the Inca Empire governed 10 million people and included parts of the present day countries of Peru, Bolivia, Colombia, Argentina, Ecuador, and Chile.

Use maps, atlases, and resource books to complete the map activities on the following page.

The Inca Empire *(cont.)*

1. Locate and label Pacific Ocean.

2. Locate these ancient cities: Cuzco, Machu Picchu.

3. Add and label the following: the Equator, the Amazon River, the Andes Mountain Range, Lake Titicaca, the Urubamba and Ucayali rivers.

4. Add a compass. Shade in the area representing the Inca Empire.

5. Trace the outline of the Inca Empire on another sheet of paper. Draw in the boundaries of the countries that exist there today. Label these countries and find their capital cities.

6. Compare the ancient and modern maps. What is the same? What was changed?

Extra Credit: What do the flags look like for each country? What do the symbols and colors represent?

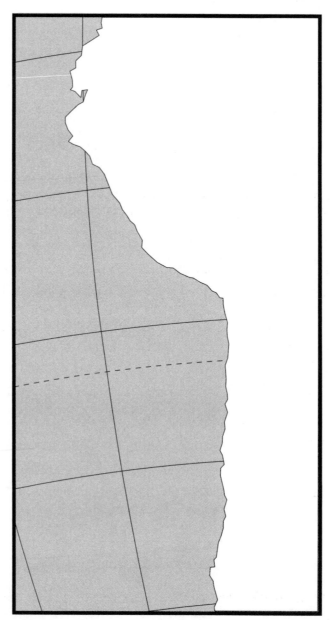

Double Talk

In *Secret of the Andes* many of the characters give advice, hints and information to Cusi through word riddles, or figures of speech. At first Cusi is confused about the meaning of these expressions. Explain what each saying really means, and what Cusi learns from it. The chapter where you can locate each quotation is given in parenthesis.

1. "Curiosity can leap the highest wall: an open gate is better." (Chapter 1)

   _____

   _____

2. "The other one did not return? . . . Death has no returning." (Chapter 6)

   _____

   _____

3. "No one who has not a drop of blood not Indian can manage a llama. The llama remembers . . ." (Chapter 7)

   _____

   _____

4. "Is your heart going back over the trail your feet have traveled?" (Chapter 8)

   _____

   _____

5. "Your acts obey only the voice of your own heart's whisper." (Chapter 9)

   _____

   _____

6. "Young birds look down from the nest only when they are nearly ready to fly." (Chapter 10)

   _____

   _____

7. "The rivers of Cuzco lie hidden beneath the cobblestones of its streets. Likewise the ways of our Ancients flow in steady streams beneath the surface of our days." (Chapter 14)

   _____

   _____

8. "Grieve not if your searching circles." (Chapter 15)

   _____

   _____

The Lost City of Machu Picchu

In 1911 Hiram Bingham discovered the ruins of the Inca mountain city of Machu Picchu. Read the following newspaper story about that discovery. You, as editor of the newspaper, are responsible for proofreading the story before the deadline. Use the editing marks at the bottom of the page to make any corrections before it goes to the typesetter to be printed.

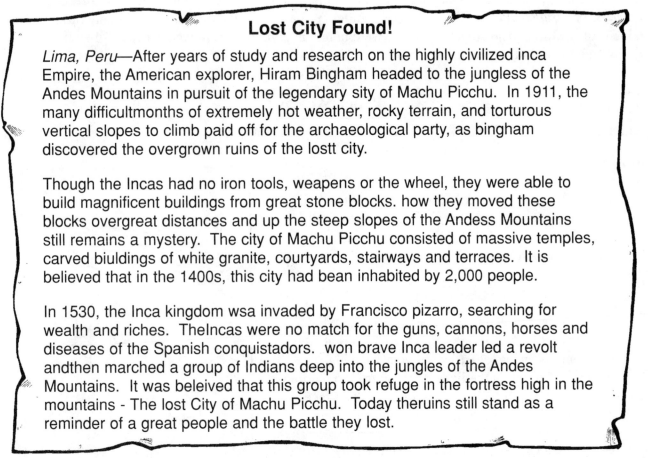

Lost City Found!

Lima, Peru—After years of study and research on the highly civilized inca Empire, the American explorer, Hiram Bingham headed to the jungless of the Andes Mountains in pursuit of the legendary sity of Machu Picchu. In 1911, the many difficultmonths of extremely hot weather, rocky terrain, and torturous vertical slopes to climb paid off for the archaeological party, as bingham discovered the overgrown ruins of the lostt city.

Though the Incas had no iron tools, weapons or the wheel, they were able to build magnificent buildings from great stone blocks. how they moved these blocks overgreat distances and up the steep slopes of the Andess Mountains still remains a mystery. The city of Machu Picchu consisted of massive temples, carved biuldings of white granite, courtyards, stairways and terraces. It is believed that in the 1400s, this city had bean inhabited by 2,000 people.

In 1530, the Inca kingdom wsa invaded by Francisco pizarro, searching for wealth and riches. TheIncas were no match for the guns, cannons, horses and diseases of the Spanish conquistadors. won brave Inca leader led a revolt andthen marched a group of Indians deep into the jungles of the Andes Mountains. It was beleived that this group took refuge in the fortress high in the mountains - The lost City of Machu Picchu. Today theruins still stand as a reminder of a great people and the battle they lost.

Editing Symbols

capital letter	≡
put in space	#
spelling error	*sp.*
paragraph	¶
delete	ℓ

Proofreading Example:

today the remains stillstand as a reminder of a grate people and the battle they they lost

Inca Weaving

The llama was the only domesticated animal of the Inca Empire. The male llamas were used for pack animals, while female llamas were sheared for their wool. Wild vicuña and alpacas wool was more valuable since those animals were much more difficult to catch and shear. After shearing, wool was spun with hand-held spindles into long threads of yarn. These threads were woven on wooden weaving bars, using a shuttle to thread the yarns over and under to create patterns, and made into blankets, *ponchos,* or *serapes.* Patterns were simple parallel, V-shaped, or diagonal stripes of many different colors. Inca women, and sometimes men, were taught at a young age to weave beautiful cloth for their family's clothing and for trading and bartering.

Paper Weaving

Materials: 12" x 18" (30 cm x 45 cm) construction paper, scissors, glue

Directions:

1. Choose a background color. Fold the paper in half vertically. Draw a line one inch (2.5 cm) from the edge opposite the folded side. This paper is the *loom,* a support structure for weaving.

2. Draw straight or wavy lines from the folded edge to the one-inch (2.5 cm) line. Space your lines at different distances for variety in your weaving patterns. Cut along the lines from the fold to the line. Open the paper and place it flat on a work surface. The vertical paper strips are called the warp.

3. Cut ¹/₂-inch (1.25 cm) strips for weaving *(weft)* from one or more contrasting pieces of paper.

4. Choose a weaving strip. Starting on one side, slide this strip alternately under and over to create a weave. Select a second strip and reverse the order. Push this strip as close as possible to the first one. Continue weaving strips until the first paper is full. This finished woven surface is called the *woof.*

5. Trim the ends, if necessary, and glue them down.

Inca Weaving *(cont.)*

Yarn Weaving

Materials: 6" x 8" inch (15 cm x 20 cm) pieces of sturdy cardboard cardboard, yarn or string, variety of yarns for weaving (different thicknesses and colors), other weaving materials (tinsel, pipe cleaners, fabric, strips, ribbon, raffia, etc.), rulers, shuttle needles

Directions:

1. Draw a line across the cardboard ½ inch (1.25 cm) from the top and botttom edges. Measure and draw vertical lines at ½ inch (1.25 cm) intervals between the horizontal lines and the top and bottom edges. Cut along these lines only to the horizontal line to form slits.

2. Tie a knot in one end of a 10' to 12' (3 m to 3.65 m) piece of yarn and insert it into one of the corner slits. Draw the string down to the first bottom slit, loop it around the back and bring it to the front through the next slit. Draw the string to the next top slit and proceed as before. Continue until all the slits are filled. When you get to the last slit, tie a knot. This is the *warp,* or foundation for your weaving.

3. You will have yarn wrapped around both sides of the cardboard loom. Weave on one side only. Choose yarns and other materials you will use to create your pattern. Thread a yarn needle with the first color you want to use or wrap a small amount around a bobbin. Take a ruler and place it under the first warp thread and over the second one.* Continue until the row is complete, and then stand the ruler on its edge and move it to the middle of the loom. This creates a shed and makes it easier to weave. Tie your *weft* (weaving thread) to the first warp string. Run it under the raised warp strings. Remove the ruler and weave it in the opposite direction over the first warp thread, under the second, and stand it on its edge. Pass the weft thread under the warp threads. Repeat this process of alternating the shed and passing the weft until the loom is filled. Watch the tension so the threads are not too tight or too loose. Use the ruler to push each line close to the last one.

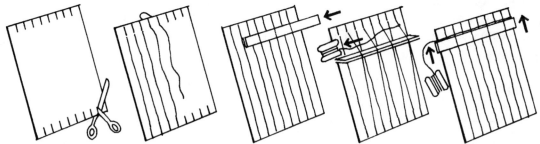

You may go over and under one thread at a time, or in groups of two or three for different patterns.

4. When your woof is finished, turn over the cardboard loom. Cut the two middle warp strings at the center and tie them together at the top and the bottom, close to the first row of weaving. Continue cutting and tying off the warp strings to the left and the right of the middle. (If you end up with three strings at the end, just tie them all together.)

5. When all the warp strings have been cut, remove the weaving from the cardboard loom. Trim the edge strings evenly to make a fringe.

The Llama

Use the following facts about the llama and its relatives to write a paragraph about the animal. Your paragraph should consist of the following:

- a topic sentence
- supporting sentences (3 to 5)
- a concluding sentence

Choose the sentences you want, or write your own sentences.

Llamas can carry loads up to 100 pounds.
Llamas are native to the continent of South America.
They are too delicate for harder jobs such as plowing.
Dried llama dung is used for fuel.
Llama meat is eaten sometimes in stews or soups.
The llama is a large woolly animal related to the camel.
They can be sheared for wool which is used to make clothing.
Their hides are made into leather for ropes and sandals.
The llama was sacred to the Incas and sometimes sacrificed to the gods in special ceremonies.
All species are able to go long periods without water.
There are four species found in South America: The guanaco and the vicuna are wild, and llamas and alpacas are domesticated by the Incas.
The shape of the llama can be found in pottery, jars, and weaving patterns.
Llamas will spit or sit down stubbornly when aggravated.

new fact:

_____

_____

new fact:

_____

_____

Choose a way to present your written work. Here are some ideas:

picture & paragraph
shape book or page
pop-up book or page

Inca Word Problems

Read the information about the Inca Empire and then use the numbers to help you solve the problems. Show all the steps it took to solve the problem and write your answers with the right label.

1. The Inca Empire lasted from about A.D. 1200 to 1532.

   a. How many years did the Empire last? _____

   _____

   b. How long has it been since the Inca Empire ended? ____

   _____

3. Above the city of Cuzco, there was a fortress called *Sacsahuaman* (which means "high-grouped-to-attack-which-provides-corpses-for-vultures"). Archaeologists believe it took 20,000 men 60 years to build this fortress.

   How long would it have taken to build if the number of workers was doubled to 40,000?

   _____

2. The capital city was Cuzco. It consisted of many stone buildings, courtyards, temples, and terraced levels. Each temple wall was made of a large number of stones perfectly fit together without any type of mortar. Each wall weighed as much as 200 tons.

   If you had a temple built in the following shape, how much would the walls weigh altogether?

   a. triangle? _____

   b. octagon? _____

   c. square? _____

   d. quadrilateral? _____

4. The Incas did not use the wheel. They had no wagons, carts or coaches—only llamas to transport goods. But the Incas did have one of the most advanced road systems in the world. Stone roads and rope bridges connected all the cities within the Empire. Relay messengers called chasquis ran over these roads, carrying information. Messages could travel the 1,250 miles (2,012 km) from Quito to Cuzco in five days!

   a. How many miles (km) per day did the messengers average? _____
   b. Llamas travel 12 ½ miles (20 km) a day. How many days would it take transport goods from Cuzco to Quito by llama?____

   _____

5. The Inca Empire stretched throughout the Andes Mountains range. Do some research to find two number facts about the Andes Mountains. Use the information to write two word problems on the back of this paper. Give your problems to another classmate to solve.

Myths, Legends, and Fables

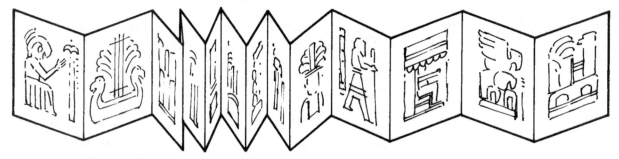

Since the beginning of time, people have tried to understand how and why the world came to be and the meaning of events in nature. Even before there was written language, these stories were told and repeated, passing from one generation to the next as oral tradition. Even though the Spanish conquerors destroyed the books and temples of the Maya, Aztecs, and Inca, the oral tradition continued, and the ancient stories are still told today. Because these stories can help to explain the beliefs and customs of past cultures, modern scholars are collecting and preserving them in books. There are several types of traditional stories.

Myths are stories told to explain how the world began, why people exist and why they die, who placed the stars in the sky, and hundreds of other questions. Myths often play an important role in religious rites and the faith of people. Examples of the most common themes of myths include:

the birth and genealogy of gods—*the myth of the fifth sun*
stories of gifts given to humankind by the gods—*Quetzalcoatl (the feathered serpent) brought civilization to the Toltecs.*
regularly occurring natural phenomena—*Huizilopochtli battles the stars and moon each night.*
stories of heroes—*Manco Capac, son of the Sun god, founded the Inca Empire.*

Legends are stories based on historic events or individuals, which have been retold and elaborated upon until it is impossible to tell how much of it really happened. An example is the legend of the lost treasure of the Inca.

Fables are short stories, often about animals that talk and act like human beings. The animals in a fable demonstrate human weaknesses in order to teach a useful lesson. Many of these lessons are as true today as they were for the ancient people. The best known are Aesop's fables. Many Aztec and Maya myths have been collected and published. See page 79 for sources.

Read traditional Maya, Aztec and Inca myths and stories to the class. Try to include a myth, a legend, and a fable.

Discuss each story as it is read, answering the following questions:

1. Is this a myth, fable, or legend?
2. What natural or historic event do you think this story is describing?
3. Can you think of another similar story that you have heard?
4. Why was this story important to the people who told it?
5. Create a picture to represent this story.
6. How does it help you understand the people who told it?

Myths, Legends, and Fables *(cont.)*

Activity

Teacher Notes: Allow several class sessions for this activity. You may limit this activity to Central and South American materials or include myths from other cultures.

1. Provide a variety of resources on myths, legends, and fables. If possible, take the class to the school library or another local library. Locate books of myths, fables, and historical legends to check out as references.

2. Provide individual copies of the chart below or draw one on the board and have the students make their own.

3. Read one story orally to the class. Model how to complete the chart by filling in the answers for the first story as a large group. Use a large piece of butcher paper, the chalkboard, or an overhead projector to show the chart.

   a. Divide the class into small groups of four or five students. Have them take turns reading another story to each other. Each group should work together to fill in their charts.

   b. Next, divide the class into partners. Have them take turns reading a third story to their partners. The partners should work together to complete their charts.

   c. For the last story, have students read on their own, then complete the chart.

4. Review all the stories by having the students report orally to the class information about the stories they read or create picture books. Have each student illustrate and write a summary of his/her favorite myth, legend, or fable. Put all the pages together to make a class book. Have a contest to design the cover. Donate the finished book to your school or a local library.

Story Chart

Title	Myth, fable or legend?	Where the story comes from	Characters	Setting	Brief summary of the story	Moral or natural events explained

Rewriting History

How would our world be affected today if certain events in history had turned out differently? Choose one of the events listed below, and write a story telling how things might have happened then, and what effect, if any, you think this would have on our lives today.

What if . . .

1. . . . Christopher Columbus had not sailed west in 1492?

2. . . . the Mayan civilization had used the wheel?

3. . . . the Inca empire had not built bridges to span the Andes mountains?

4. . . . Hernando Cortés had arrived on foot and with bows, arrows, and spears instead of on horseback with gunpowder?

5. . . . the Mayan mathematicians had not created the symbol for zero?

6. . . . a virus had destroyed the Inca potato crop, or drought had destroyed the Aztec and Mayan corn crops?

7. . . . Chinese explorers had sailed across the Pacific Ocean and invaded the Aztec empire?

8. . . . dinosaurs had still existed during these three pre-Columbian civilizations?

9. . . . Doña Marina and Hernando Cortés had become Emperor and Empress of the Aztec empire?

10. . . . there had been a strong Sapa Inca when Pizarro reached Peru?

11. Your idea—What if . . .

Pyramid Poetry

Step 1—*Preparation*

1. Show pictures of pre-Columbian pyramids and Egyptian pyramids. Discuss the differences and similarities. (Main points: pre-Columbian pyramids were step construction and used for religious ceremonies while Egyptian pyramids were flat-side construction and used as tombs.)

2. Divide a chalkboard or large piece of butcher paper into two sections. Ask the students to come to the board in small groups and have each student write one word that can be used to describe a pre-Columbian pyramid on one side. Have dictionaries and thesauruses available to help fill the board with as many words as possible. As the students finish, discuss the words, erase duplicates, edit for spelling and capital letters, etc.

Step 2—*Writing*

1. Select one of the forms below and write the pattern on the second half of the board or paper. Using the words the students brainstormed, demonstrate how to write a poem. Ask students to suggest other variations.

2. Have the students write rough drafts of their poems on a piece of lined paper. (If you wish, the students may choose their own forms—rhyming, free style, haiku, etc.) Exchange poems with partners for editing. Have volunteers read their poems in class.

Cinquain	**Tanka**
Line 1: the name of your subject	Line 1: five syllables
Line 2: two adjectives	Line 2: seven syllables
Line 3: three nouns	Line 3: five syllables
Line 4: two verbs	Line 4: seven syllables
Line 5: synonym for your subject	Line 5: seven syllables

Step 3—*Presentation*

Make an enlarged copy of the step pyramid and a copy for each student. Fill the steps with their poems. Cut them out and put them together in a class book. Donate your class book to the school library.

Extension: Follow the steps to generate ideas and vocabulary about other topics related to Central and South American cultures.

Pyramid Poetry *(cont.)*

Pyramid Writing Form

Mayan Math

The ancient Maya were one of only three civilizations to discover and use the concept of zero. Although their system used only three symbols, the Maya were able to measure time and record dates with great accuracy. Zero in the Mayan system, and in ours, shows the place value of numbers.

The Maya based their number system on 20, which probably came from using fingers and toes to count objects. Archaeologists believe that the Maya moved from counting with fingers and toes to using cocoa beans and bean pods on counting boards, which probably looked like boxes in a column. Five beans would be exchanged for one pod. When the box contained three pods (15) and 4 beans, the box was cleared, and one bean was added to the box on top. It was very easy to see the numbers in this way. This probably also explains why the Maya wrote their numbers vertically. (In our system, we move from right to left to indicate place value.)

Later, when they wanted to carve numbers on monuments, there was a problem. How would they know whether the single dot (or bean) meant 1 or 20 if it was removed from the box? To solve this dilemma, they invented a symbol that looks like a shell (or a closed fist) to show that a box is empty. This is similar to the way that zero works in our number system. Zero allows us to see the difference between 1 and 10. In Mayan math, the shell tells us whether the dot represents 1 or 20.

Activity

Mayan Counting

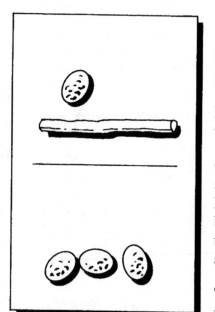

Materials: beans, cinnamon sticks, macaroni shells, 3" x 8" (7.5 cm x 20 cm) strips of heavy paper divided into 4 equal boxes

Directions: Divide the class into teams or small groups. Give each team a supply of beans, sticks, and shells and a counting board.

One student will count the beans while the other serves as recorder and banker. As the beans are counted, the recorder draws the missing Mayan numerals on the chart. When the counter has placed five beans in the box, he/she exchanges them for a cinnamon stick. When the box has three sticks and four beans, replace them with a shell and add a bean to the next box up.

Teacher Note: Full lesson plans and additional activities are presented in *Maya Math*, from Sunburst Communications.

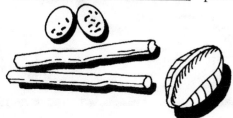

More Mayan Math

You have seen that the Maya used just three symbols and that they never showed more than three bars and four dots in any one place. You have also seen that this system is vertical.

At the lowest level, each dot is one and each bar is five. This box can hold a total of 19. _____

In the next box, each dot represents 20. What does each bar represent? _____

What is the highest number that can be written using the first and second boxes?_____

The third box begins where the second one ends. One dot in the third box means 400.

Follow the example to translate these Mayan numbers into our numbers.

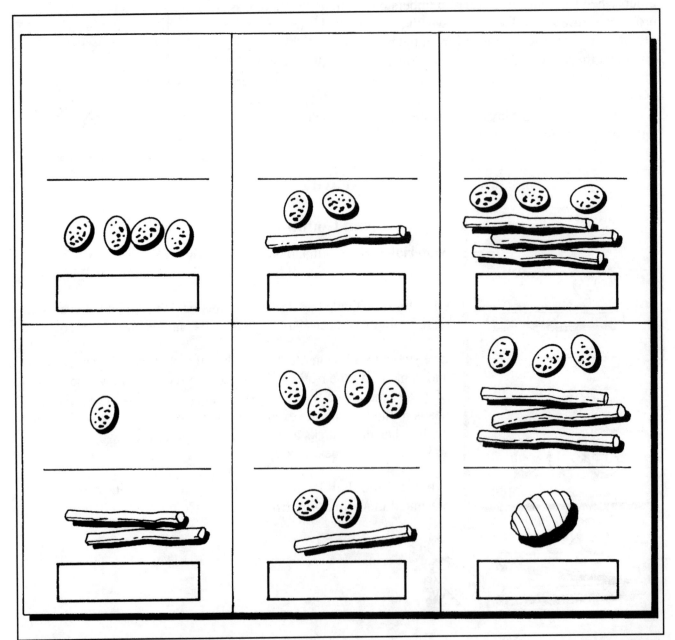

Aztec Battle Shields

War was a way of life for the pre-Columbian Aztecs. Their religion, ceremonies, social structure, schooling, and even the way they dressed reflected the importance of the warrior.

The Aztecs were never too young to train for war. It started with a special ceremony at the birth of a baby boy. At the age of six, boys entered *telpochcalli*, a school of military training. At the age of ten, they became warriors. When a warrior had captured or killed four prisoners, he then could become an Aztec *tequina*, or citizen. The highest honor for a warrior was to become a jaguar or eagle knight.

Aztec warriors used round shields made of reeds or wood. They were decorated with feathers, mosaics, or metal ornaments. This shield was called a *chimalli*. Shields were used in battle or given as gifts and used for trading. Shield designs were as unique as each warrior. They were designed with symbols that showed the warrior's rank and feats of bravery. The shields were painted with natural dyes using bright colors of red, white, yellow-gold, green, black, and blue. Warriors also used black obsidian blades to make a variety of weapons like small knives, and long, sharp spears called *macuahiutl*.

Make an Aztec Battle Shield

Materials: paper plates (1 per student), plain drawing paper, crayons, markers or paint, scissors and glue, scraps of fabric, colored paper, foil, feathers, glitter, beads, yarn, tissue and crepe paper, etc.

1. Research library and classroom books for some ideas and patterns. Jaguars, eagles, and serpents were highly respected symbols. Bright colors, feathers, metals (like gold and silver), and mosaics made from semiprecious stones (like turquoise) were used frequently.

2. On a piece of plain paper, trace the shape of the paper plate. Plan your designs, deciding what colors, symbols, and art techniques you want to use.

3. Using pencil, draw your design on the paper plate. Add color.

4. Add extra items like dangling feathers, colored paper cut into mosaic pieces, or pieces of foil.

5. On the back of your shield, write a paragraph explaining what the symbols and colors you used represent. Create a classroom display of battle shields.

Cultural Time Line

To help understand the development of the ancient cultures of America, make a time line showing their growth, and the growth of other areas of the world. This time line will help students compare more familiar events to new knowledge and develop historical perspective.

Determine how much space there is for the time line. It should be large enough to allow students to add events, and read them easily.

Begin by measuring and marking a narrow column of dates on the left. The scope of this time line is 3,500 BC to A.D. 1620. Divide the remaining paper into four columns. Label the columns from left to right: Europe, Near East and Asia, Central America and Mexico, Peru.

Year	Europe	Near East and Asia	Central America and Mexico	Peru
B.C. 3500		First Egyptian dynasty founded		
B.C. 3000	Beginning of Minoan Age in Crete			
B.C. 2000			First farm settlements in Guatemala, Chiapas, Yucatan	
B.C. 1200				Chavin civilization in highlands, Coastal settlements

As you explore the civilizations of Peru, Mexico, and Central America, add significant dates to the columns. Find the founding dates of cities, births of great rulers, dates of conquests and ending dates for periods of history.

Transfer the information below to the appropriate columns on the chart.

Europe
B.C.
3000 Beginning of Minoan Age in Crete
776 First Oylmpic Games in Greece
734 Legendary founding of Rome
27 Caesar Augustus crowned first Roman Emperor
A.D.
410 Fall of Rome
800 Charlemagne crowned Holy Roman Empire
1066 William the Conqueror invades England
1215 Magna Carta signed in England
1400 The Renaissance begins
1439 Printing invented
1588 English defeat Spanish Armada
1620 England sends colonists to North America

Near East and Asia
B.C.
3500 First Egyptian dynasty founded
2700 Chinese civilization begins
326 Alexander the Great conquers Near East
210 Great Wall of China built
A.D.
632 Beginning of Arab Empire
1206–1221 Ghengis Khan conquers central Asia and China
1389 Turks invade Europe
1369–1405 Tamerlane rules Asia
1519–1522 Magellan sails around the world

Central America and Mexico
B.C.
2000 First farm settlements in Guatemala, Chiapas, Yucatan
1500 Olmec Civilization
300 Rise of the Maya begins
150 Teotihuacan settled by farmers
A.D.
100 Pyramids built at Teotihuacan

Peru
B.C.
1200 Chavin civilization in highlands, Coastal settlements
100 Moche kingdom on the Northern coast, Nazca ruled the south
A.D.
800 Tiahuanaco captures the southern coast

The Sun . . . Fiction

Because the lives of early people in Central America depended on the forces of nature, they worshipped gods who personified the sun and rain, which were necessary for crops. Ancient astronomers studied the heavenly bodies and learned to tell time and predict eclipses of the sun and moon. Their calendars were based on solar and lunar observation. The Aztecs thought of themselves as the sun's people. Their entire religion was based upon the sun's cycle of rising and setting. The many Aztec rituals and ceremonies were designed around this cycle of the sun. They believed that without their rituals and ceremonies, this cycle would stop and the world would end.

The Spanish conquistadors who conquered the Aztecs were shocked when they witnessed the rituals of human sacrifice. Archaeologists have struggled to understand the importance of these sacrifices and their meaning in Aztec life. The Aztecs believed that they had to feed the sun with human blood. The ritual victims were often captured slaves or prisoners of war. They were costumed and well-treated, feasted, and then sacrificed on a temple altar. These victims were called the "children of the sun." It was considered an honor to be able to join the gods. These rituals also created a cycle. More wars were waged for more prisoners, for more sacrifices, for more honor to the sun.

The Aztecs made mosaic masks of precious metals and stones, such as turquoise, to honor the sun god. These masks were worn for many of the daily ceremonies the Aztecs followed.

Make a Sun God Mask

Materials: piece of cardboard, string or yarn (any color), foil, glue and scissors, permanent markers, tape, optional—feathers, sequins, raffia, yarn, glitter, etc.

Directions:

1. Draw an oval shape on the cardboard and cut it out.

2. Draw your face design on the cardboard.

3. Glue string over your design. Let it dry overnight.

4. Cover the mask with foil. Tape the foil down on the back. Press the foil gently with your fingertips until your design becomes visible. Be careful! Foil can tear easily with fingernails and rings.

5. Using permanent markers, color your mask. Remember, permanent means permanent. Be careful!

6. Add extras like feathers, sequins, raffia, yarn, glitter, etc.

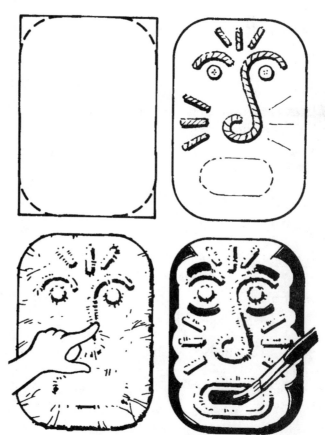

The Sun: . . . Facts

Today we know that the sun is an average-sized star, made of hot gases. These hot gases, mostly hydrogen and helium, explode with energy continuously. This energy flows out from the center of the sun and escapes into space. The Earth and other planets receive the sun's energy as heat, light and other forms of radiation.

The sun is the closest star to our planet. It is 93,000,000 miles (149,730,000 km) away! Light from the sun takes about eight minutes to reach us, so we actually see the sun as it was eight minutes ago.

The hottest part of the sun is the core, or center. The core can reach temperatures up to 57,000,000° F (31,666,648 C)! This tremendous heat from the core is sent to the surface through the middle and outer layers. The *photosphere* is the surface, or outside layer, of the sun. Here there are dark spots that may grow or disappear; these are called *sunspots*. Flares are powerful explosions, lasting only a few seconds, that occur on or between sunspots. Sometimes huge sheets of glowing gases can be seen leaping from the photosphere. These are called *prominences*, and they can reach 250,000 miles (40,250,000 km) into the sky. The *chromosphere* is a bright, reddish-pink area of very, very hot gases around the sun. The layer of atmosphere around the sun is the *corona*, it creates the white-yellowish "color" of the sun.

The diameter of the sun, or distance across it is 109 times greater than the Earth's diameter. You can fit about one million Earths inside the Sun!

Vocabulary Review

Match each word to its best definition

_____ 1. hydrogen and helium

_____ 2. core

_____ 3. photosphere

_____ 4. prominences

_____ 5. diameter

_____ 6. conquer

_____ 7. conquistadors

_____ 8. rituals

_____ 9. solar year

_____ 10. mosaic

a. a cycle of 365 days

b. the distance across a circle

c. special celebrations

d. the center

e. another name for Spanish explorers

f. the surface, or outside layer of the sun

g. a work of art created from small pieces of stone, metal, tile, etc.

h. leaping sheets of glowing gases on the photosphere of the sun

i. to take control of a group of people

j. gases

Make a Solar Cooker

The energy produced by the sun is tremenduous. Today many people are trying to find ways to convert the heat of the sun into power.

Materials: empty, cylindrical oatmeal box; aluminum foil; clean wire coat hanger; hot dog, bright, sunny day

Directions:

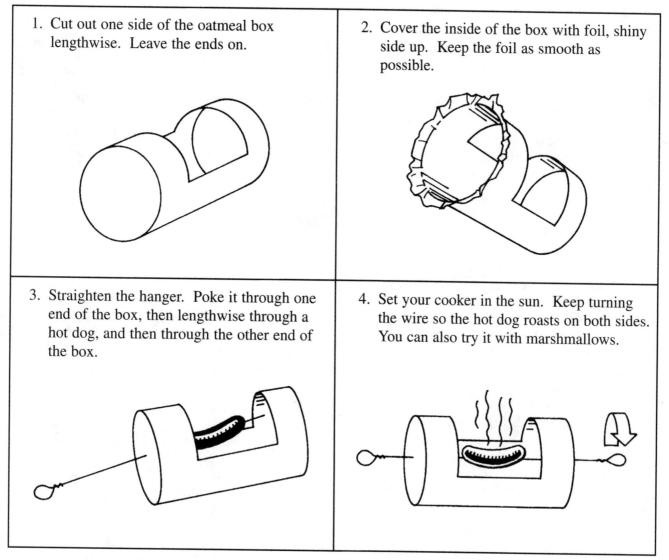

1. Cut out one side of the oatmeal box lengthwise. Leave the ends on.

2. Cover the inside of the box with foil, shiny side up. Keep the foil as smooth as possible.

3. Straighten the hanger. Poke it through one end of the box, then lengthwise through a hot dog, and then through the other end of the box.

4. Set your cooker in the sun. Keep turning the wire so the hot dog roasts on both sides. You can also try it with marshmallows.

Why It Works:

The curved foil acts as a solar reflector. It focuses the heat of the sun on your hot dog. You save energy by sizzling your hot dog with the sun instead of using electricity or some other source of fuel.

Extension: Brainstorm a list of other ways that the power of the sun can (and is) used to replace traditional fuels. Research one use of solar power or think of a new way to use this energy source. Share your findings or invention with the class.

Mayan Food and Recipes

The Maya were farmers living in the tropical jungles of Mexico, Guatemala, and Belize. They used stone axes to remove trees and clear the land for farming. By causing friction with a wooden drill, they could burn away the remaining thick brush. This method was called slash and burn. The fire ash would be left as a fertilizer, but the land was still poor. After a few years the field would be abandoned, and the farmer would clear new land. The old fields would be left to return to jungle growth.

The main crop of the Maya was maize, or corn. Beans would be planted in the same hole as the corn, which would support the beans as they grew. Maize kernels soaked in limewater were ground on carved stones called *metates*. Then the moist dough was formed by hand into thin pancakes called *tortillas* and baked on a hot, flat stone. The *tortilla* would be filled with vegetables and spices, rolled up, and eaten. Meat was sometimes added on special occasions.

The Maya also grew cotton, tobacco, sweet potatoes, cocoa beans, squash, gourds, chili peppers, tomatoes, pumpkins, turnips, and henequen, a plant used to make rope. They planted orchards of avocado trees to provide necessary protein in their diets. Papayas, bananas, nuts, and plantains, a type of banana, could be found in the wild. Maya also kept hives of bees in hollow logs for a steady supply of honey. People living near the coasts caught and dried fish and traded salt.

Activities

Grow Indian Corn

1. Place a cob of Indian corn in a shallow tray.

2. Add enough warm water to cover the lower half of the cob.

3. Place the tray in a warm place but not direct sunlight. Leave it for a few days.

4. When the kernels begin to sprout, move the tray to a place with sunlight. Add or change the water as necessary.

5. After watching the sprouts grow, you can . . .

   a. gently pull the sprouts off and plant them in a class garden.

   b. plant them in a paper cup with soil and watch them grow more.

   c. eat them!

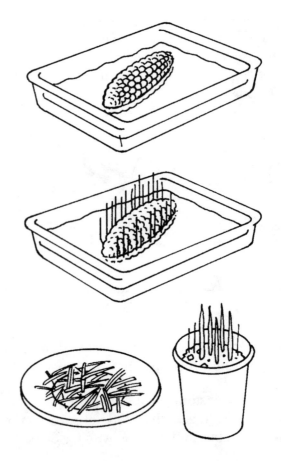

Mayan Food and Recipes *(cont.)*

Make Your Own Tortillas

Ingredients:

- 2 ½ cups (600 ml) corn flour or masa harina, found in the Mexican grocery section
- 1 cup (.24 l) warm water
- rolling pin
- waxed paper
- heavy frying pan

Directions:

1. Combine the corn flour and warm water in a large mixing bowl. Using wet hands, mix the dough until you can form it into a large ball (add small amounts of water, if necessary).

2. Wet hands again and shape the dough into 12 smaller balls (about the size of a golf ball).

3. Put one ball onto a piece of waxed paper. Place another piece of waxed paper on top. Roll with a rolling pin until it is about 6 inches (15 cm) in diameter. Continue for each ball of dough.

4. Heat the ungreased frying pan to medium-hot.

5. Peel off the top sheet of wax paper. Flip over and drop tortilla (paper side up) into the frying pan. Peel off the remaining paper. Cook for 30 seconds. Turn and cook for one minute. Turn and cook for 30 seconds. Tortillas should be soft and dry with light brown flecks.

6. To serve:

   a. brush with butter, sprinkle with cinnamon and sugar

   b. sprinkle with grated cheese, broil until melted

   c. add taco meat, cheese, and lettuce

   d. add warm refried beans, and roll up

Aztec Food and Recipes

The Aztecs ate a variety of foods. The most important staple was maize, or corn. It was eaten raw, or roasted on hot stones. Other main foods were beans, seeds, wild plants, and insects (such as ants and agave worms). The many different soils and climates of the area provided a wide variety of fruits and vegetables, some even grown on floating mud and reed gardens called *chimampas*. Papayas, avocados, peppers, mangoes, guavas, chiles, sweet and white potatoes, tomatoes, and fruits of the cacti were all available. The *maguey*, a fruit of the agave cactus, was used for many things. The seeds were roasted and used for seasoning, the pulp was mashed and put in tortillas, the thorns made sewing needles, the stringy fibers were used for weaving, and the liquid made a powerful alcoholic beverage called *pulque*.

Meat consisted of game animals such as pheasants, ducks, deer, boars, bears and their two domesticated animals, turkeys and dogs (seldom served). They also enjoyed many water animals like frogs, tadpoles, turtles, shrimp, waterflies, and waterfly eggs served like caviar.

The foods were highly spiced and covered with a variety of sauces, made from sage, peppers, tomatoes, and pimentos. During excavations in modern Mexico, archaeologists uncovered a recipe for a royal sauce served at the table of the Aztec kings. It takes three days to prepare and has the following ingredients: four kinds of peppers, garlic, cinnamon, cloves, black peppers, caraway and sesame seeds, raisins, almonds, peanuts, onion and . . . chocolate! (to thicken the sauce and give it taste and color).

Chocolate is made from cacao beans. These beans were so highly prized that they were even used as currency for bartering. While most Aztecs drank water, rich families and royalty drank a chocolate drink called *xocoatl*. The emperor Montezuma loved the chocolate drink and is said to have drunk as many as 50 cups a day! This required large quantities of cacao beans. When Cortés arrived at Tenochititlan, one of Montezuma's warehouses contained over 2,000,000 pounds (900,000 kg) of cacao beans. Cortés introduced chocolate to Europe, where it was sweetened with sugar and vanilla (also from the New World) into the chocolate we know today.

Aztec Food and Recipes *(cont.)*

Activities

Make Aztec Hot Chocolate (Xocoatl)

This recipe can be made at a large table in rotating groups of three students.

Ingredients:

4 tablespoons (60 ml) powdered cocoa

3 tablespoons (45 ml) honey

1 teaspoon (5 ml) vanilla

1 teaspoon (5 ml) cinnamon

1 ½ cups (.36 l) milk

1 ½ cups (.36 l) boiling water

(An electric kettle works well in the classroom.)

Directions:

1. Measure and mix all the ingredients into a medium-size bowl.
2. Beat with a hand-held mixer until frothy.
3. Pour into cups and enjoy!

   (How is this different from the hot chocolate you are familiar with?)
4. Clean up the area for the next group.

Make an Aztec Restaurant Menu

1. Fold a 12" x 18" (30 x 45 cm) piece of construction paper into thirds.

2. Decide on a name for your restaurant, like *Tehuacan's Eatery* or the *Quetzalcoatl Café*. Design a logo using the name you have selected and draw it across the top of the middle section.

3. Divide your menu into food categories like appetizers, main courses, desserts, salads, beverages, etc., and write those titles.

4. Create your own dishes for each category, using only Aztec foods. Carefully write the name of the dish with a brief description of the ingredients, like *Teotehuacan Treats: Grilled fresh ants in a delicate chocolate and peanut sauce.*

5. Add colorful illustrations and designs. For each dish, list a price—in cacao beans!

Inca Food and Recipes

The Incas were great farmers and created an ingenious way to farm in the steep mountains of the Andes. They needed to use every piece of available land in order to feed the country. Along the fertile river valleys, they made channels to divert water to irrigate the crops. Much of Peru is mountainous, making it difficult to grow crops. The Incas constructed terraces, or steps, in the mountainside to create flat spaces on which to plant. Canals were built to bring water down the slopes to the dry areas. All this is even more remarkable when considering the Incas had no machinery or animals to help them plow. All the work was done by hand.

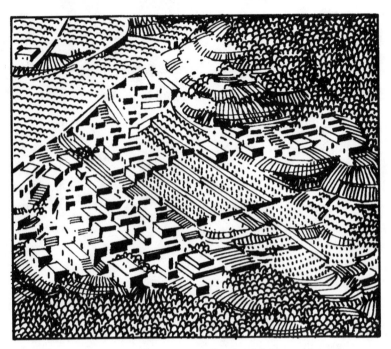

Most farmers had several fields at different altitudes or levels of the slope. In the highest elevations, they grew potatoes and other hardy crops that could survive the cold. At the middle level, they planted maize, barley, beans, peanuts, pumpkins, and *quinoa* (a grain). In the lower valleys, fruits and vegetables were grown.

The rain forest on the eastern slope of the Andes provided cacao beans. Along the coast, fishermen caught a variety of fish, from giant rays and sharks to anchovies. Most of the fishing was done with nets, using boats made of bundled reeds. The people of coastal communities also collected valuable *guano,* the droppings of seabirds, to be used as fertilizer by the farmers. Guano was so valuable that killing the birds or disturbing their nests could mean death.

Most Incas ate only two meals a day. The morning consisted of a cereal or soup. Dinner was also a soup made from potatoes and corn, quinoa, chili peppers, onions, or squash. Meat was rarely eaten. Llama or guinea pig was eaten for special occasions. The leftovers would then be made into a dried meat food called *charqui.* The English word "jerky" comes from this Inca word. The Incas also devised a method of freeze-drying potatoes so they would last for five or six years. The potatoes would be set out in the cold night air to freeze. The next day, after the potatoes had defrosted in the sun, they would be mashed (by feet) until the moisture was squeezed out. This would be repeated until the potatoes were hard white chunks. These chunks could be stored until needed, at which time they could be soaked in water and then cooked.

Perhaps the most important staple of the Inca was the white potato, which they were the first to cultivate. Spaniards returning from the New World introduced potatoes to Europe. Now this popular and nutritious food is available around the world. While most of us have seen only two or three varieties of potatoes, some villages in Peru harvest as many as 70 different kinds.

Inca Food and Recipes (cont.)

Activities

Fire-Baked Potatoes

Ingredients:

- large barbecue
- aluminum foil
- small whole potatoes
- tomatoes and pimentos

Directions:

1. Scrub the potatoes and wrap them in foil. Stick them among the coals of a fire or hot barbecue. Surround the potatoes with coals.
2. Bake about an hour, or until the potato can be pierced easily with a fork.
3. Unwrap the foil and take the potatoes out. (Be careful, they are hot!) Slice into sections. Serve with fresh sliced tomatoes and top with pimentos.

Make a Potato Head

Directions:

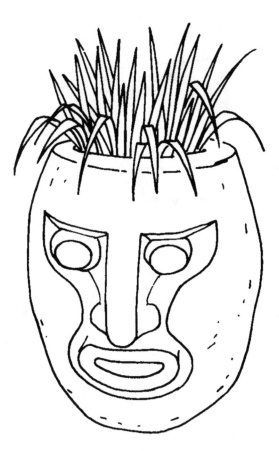

1. Use a white potato.
2. Cut off both ends to make it sit upright.
3. Use a paring knife (carefully, of course!) to carve a face on one side of the potato.
4. Use a spoon to hollow out about $\frac{1}{4}$ inch (.63 cm) in the top.
5. Fill the top with grass seed or birdseed. Water gently (or the seeds will float out) every day with a spray bottle.
6. Place in a sunny area, and in a week to 10 days "hair" will grow.

Variations:

- Some imaginative students can even get eyebrows and beards to grow!

- Add cloves for eyes, mouths, etc.

- Trim the "hair" into different styles as it grows.

Mexican Pinch Pots

Pottery has been made and used throughout Mexico and Central America since ancient times.

Show some ceramic examples to the class or visit a company where pottery is made. Bring in some examples of Mexican pottery so students can study the modern designs and colors. Have the students research the history of pottery in Mexico, and some of the historical and traditional patterns and colors. What did they use their containers for?

Materials: self-hardening or oven-firing clay; small containers of water; brushes; acrylic glazes, paints, or reddish-brown tempera paint; spray acrylic sealer

Directions:

1. Give each student a ball of clay 2 or 3 inches (5 or 7.5 cm) in diameter.
2. Prepare the clay by throwing it down on a hard surface, and then kneading out the air bubbles. This is called wedging. Repeat this several times.
3. Pat and smooth the clay into a ball. Push both thumbs together into the middle. Shape the bowl by pulling the sides out from the center and pinching with the fingers. Be careful not to pinch the sides too thin. Turn the bowl frequently so that the sides remain the same thickness.
4. When you have a shape you like, dip your fingers into water to smooth out any cracks. Let the pot dry for several days or follow the manufacturer's directions to oven fire it.
5. Paint a base coat with a reddish-brown acrylic or tempera paint. When that coat is dry, paint a design similar to the examples of Mexican pottery, using a second color. Spray the finished piece with a ceramic sealer or lacquer.

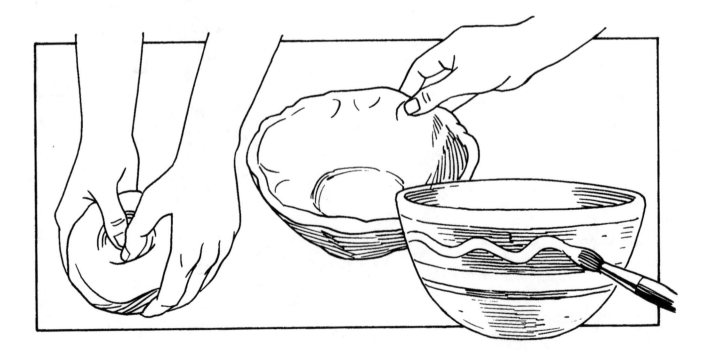

Central American Molas

Molas are an art form that uses applique. *Applique* is a method of applying one piece of fabric to another. The design is created by cutting through layers of colored cotton fabric, exposing the different colors underneath. The edges of the shapes are turned under and sewn together with tiny stitches. It was originally used in clothing, but can now be found in wall hangings and many other forms. Try the directions below to make your own paper mola.

Materials: three different colors of 9" x 12" (23 cm x 30 cm) construction paper, (one piece of each color for each student), scissors and glue

Directions:

1. Label the three pieces of construction paper A, B, and C.
2. On paper A, draw a shape outline of an animal, person, or object.
3. Using the tips of your scissors, cut into the center of your paper A, and cut along your outline.
4. Place paper A on top of paper B. Draw circles, ovals, diamonds, and stars, etc. Using the tips of your scissors, cut into the middle of these shapes and cut them out.
5. Glue the three pieces of paper together with C on the bottom, then B, and A on top.

Variations: outline the shape with yarn, add glitter to one level, or use a craft knife instead of scissors.

Paper A
Cut out outline of animal, person, or object.

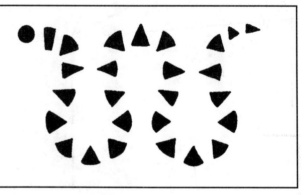

Paper B
Cut out smaller inside shapes.

Paper C

Pyramids

Use this pattern to make a pyramid. Follow the directions on the pattern. Remember to add color, lines for the steps, and designs before you glue it together. Add extras like glitter, sequins, foil, paper people figures, etc.

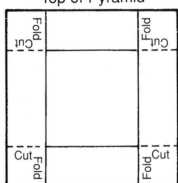

Top of Pyramid

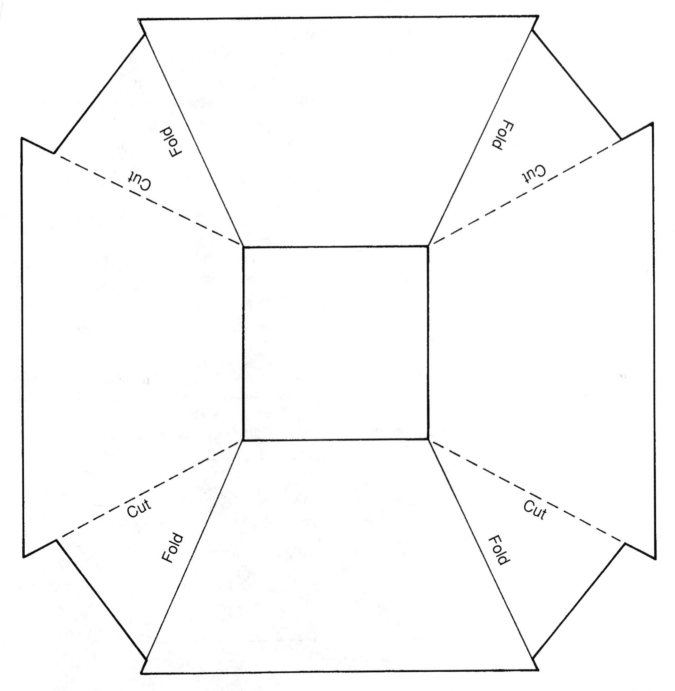

Ball Games

Pelota

There were many versions of this ball game which looked like a cross between basketball and soccer. Although the rules varied from tribe to tribe, it was a highly significant and difficult game. Winning teams were richly rewarded. The losers may have been sacrificed to the gods. Almost every archaeological site uncovered contains a ball court. Two good books to read are *Rain Player* by David Wisniewski and *A Quetzalcoatl: Tale of the Ball Game* by Marilyn Parke. Here is a simplifed version:

Materials: 2 volleyball poles, 2 hula hoops, 1 beach ball

Purpose: to hit the beach ball through the hoops without using your hands or forearms

Play: two teams of six players on a large "H" shaped court (drawn with chalk, or marked with tape)

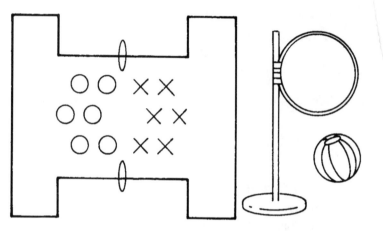

Indian Ball

The game of kickball demonstrated the endurance and skill of the players. Different types of kickball were played in local villages and on days of celebrations. Here is a simplified version of one type of kickball.

Materials: 3-inch (7.5 cm) diameter rubber ball, books, cardboard boxes and tubes to make the obstacle course, stopwatch

Purpose: to complete the obstacle course in the fastest time, using only your feet to maneuver the ball Work in relay teams of two persons each. Team members must alternate kicking the ball, working together to complete the course.

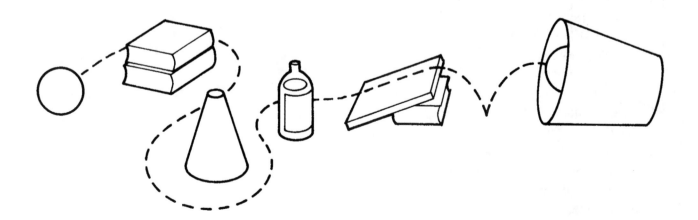

Mayan, Aztec, and Inca Figures

The Maya, Aztecs and Incas used many colorful ideas in their clothing:

❏ multicolored, geometric and/or striped materials woven from the fibers of *maguey* or the wool of llamas and alpacas

❏ feathers from birds like parrots, eagles, and quetzels

❏ animal skin from jaguars and vicunas

❏ metals, like gold, silver and, copper

❏ semiprecious gems, such as turquoise, onyx, jade, and rock crystals

❏ ponchos, serapes, headdresses, and masks

Materials: copies of the person pattern (page 75), research books, coloring materials, scissors and glue, 12" x 18" (30 cm x 46 cm) construction paper, paper scraps, foil, glitter, felt, feathers, beads, etc.

Directions:

1. Choose the type of person you will research. Select a culture, and decide what role the person has in that society. It may be a man or woman, a soldier, a noble, a common person, etc. Look in encyclopedias or research books to find details about your particular person. A great resource is the *Eyewitness Series: Aztecs, Incas and Maya.* Make a rough sketch of what the figure looks like and the names of the parts of clothing.

2. Get your materials ready. Decide what type of extras you will need to find or make.

3. Cut out the figure pattern and glue it to a piece of construction paper.

4. Add the basic pieces of clothing first. You can either draw directly onto the picture or cut out separate pieces and glue them on. Then add smaller articles of clothing, facial features, hair, and extras.

5. Label the pieces of clothing and add details like jewelry, weapons, baskets, shields, a background landscape, headdresses, feathers, beads, etc.

6. Choose a name for the person you have created and write a story about a typical day in the person's life. Glue your story to the back of the picture.

Mayan, Aztec, and Inca Figures *(cont.)*

Person Pattern

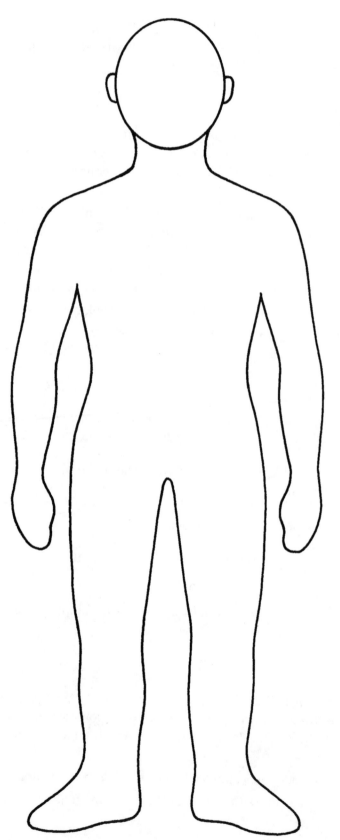

Creating Mayan, Aztec, or Inca Villages

Note to teacher: Divide the class into three or more small groups. These projects will require several work periods for planning and construction. Provide an alternative assignment and working area for those students who choose not to work in a group.

Step 1: Planning

1. As a group, decide which type of village you will build: Aztec, Mayan, or Inca. Brainstorm ideas about how you can make 3-D buildings and landscapes. On a piece of blank paper, draw a bird's eye view of your plan. Label important items. Discuss your group's plans and ideas with your teacher.

2. Once you have a plan for your village, brainstorm a list of materials you will need. Make a master list. Then assign everybody in your group items from the list that they will provide. Make individual lists to take home. Decide on a date when all materials need to be back at school. (If you have a group member who cannot bring anything in, give that student the master list and put him/her in charge of storing and organizing all the materials as the items come to school.)

   Possible materials: sturdy cardboard to build on (soft drink cardboard flat works well), paper scraps, small boxes, plastic wrap, toothpicks, sugar cubes, craft sticks, markers or crayons, colored pencils, glue, masking tape, scissors, dirt, sand, grasses, leaves, rocks, twigs, etc.

Step 2: Building the Village

Assign a job to each person. Some jobs may require more than one person. Individuals who have completed their assigned tasks may assist others or begin Step 3.

Landscaper: lays down the soil, decides where buildings should be, makes and places trees and shrubs, makes water areas (coastline, streams, lakes), builds mountains

Architect: designs and makes the buildings, temples and/or bridges

Engineer: makes all the small accessories like people, animals, pottery, weapons, baskets, blankets, fires, boats, etc.

Contractor: the person in charge, keeps materials organized and supplied, makes sure everyone is doing job, resolves arguments, researches pictures for new ideas

Step 3: Presentation

1. When the villages are finished, each group must prepare a written page of information about everyday life in their village. Each group member is responsible for researching and writing one paragraph of the final draft. Decide who will write which topics and the order of your paragraphs. Make a final draft.

2. Show your village and read your paper to the class. Each person should read his/her paragraph.

Extension: On presentation day, dress to represent the culture you are presenting. Share a treat from that culture.

Bulletin Board Ideas

Directions:

1. Cover the top one-third of the bulletin board with blue paper for the sky and the remainder with brown paper for the land. As you move from one civilization to the next, add to or change the details.

2. After introducing each culture through pictures and/or videos, have the class brainstorm things that could be found in the chosen landscape. List all the ideas on the chalkboard. Assign each student an item from the board to make. Discuss the size of the bulletin board in proportion with their items. Attach items to the board as they finish.

Maya: rain forest trees, coastline, canoes, thatched adobe houses, corn plants, gardens, stone temples, step pyramids, quetzal birds, aqueducts, reeds, sun and rain clouds, twisted crepe paper for vines, moon and stars

Aztecs: step pyramids, stone houses, statues, cacti, reeds around a lake, cooking fires, grinding stones, tall grasses, desert animals, the sun, pottery, corn plants, thatched houses

Inca: tall mountains, rope bridges from twisted brown crepe paper, llamas, potato plants, weaving

Classroom Decorations

Since ancient times the people of Mexico and Central America have used flowers as decorations. In Mexico City, brightly colored flowers grow in the flowering gardens of Xochimilco; Decorate your classroom with these flowers.

Tissue Paper Flowers

Materials: 6" x 9" (15 cm x 23 cm) pieces of tissue paper in assorted colors (six sheets per student), scissors, pipe cleaners (one per flower)

Directions:

1. Stack six sheets of tissue paper. You can mix colors, alternate colors, or use all the same color.
2. Starting with the short side, fold the tissue paper back and forth like a fan.
3. Cut the open edges in petal shapes, either round or pointed.
4. Pinch the center of the tissue paper and tie with a pipe cleaner.
5. Lift up one layer of tissue paper at a time and push toward the middle. Continue until all layers have been separated and pushed forward.

Variations: Add green tissue paper leaves, add more pipe cleaners for longer stems and put the flowers in a vase, add glitter to the center, use colored facial tissues or colored napkins instead of tissue paper, or spray lightly with perfume.

Tissue Paper Banners

Materials: assorted colors of tissue paper, 18" x 24" (46 x 61 cm), one per student; scissors; tape; string

Directions:

1. Fold the paper in half, over and over (at least five times).
2. Using scissors, make small cutouts all the way around the folded rectangle. Use any kinds of shapes, like geometrics, curves, triangles, half circles, rectangles, hearts, diamonds, etc. (This is similar to cutting patterns in snowflakes).
3. Fold the paper in half one more time, and cut one larger design in the middle.
4. Carefully unfold the paper (tissue paper rips easily). If needed, you can flatten the paper overnight under a heavy stack of books.
5. Tape banners along a string across the room or window.

Variations: Add another piece of tissue paper to the back, glue together, and then frame for a suncatcher.

Bibliography of Selected Resources

Fiction

Alexander, Lloyd. *The El Dorado Adventure.* Puffin, 2000.

Bierhorst, John. *Doctor Coyote, A Native American Aesop's Fables.* Aladdin Paperbacks, 1996.

Carlson, Lori. *Where Angels Glide at Dawn.* Econo-Clad, 1999.

Casteneda, Omar S. *Among the Volcanoes.* Learning Books, 1993.

Cherry, Lynn. *The Great Kapok Tree.* Harcourt & Brace, 1998.

Ehlert, Lois. *Moon Rope.* Harcourt Brace, 1997.

Lattimore, Deborah Nourse. *The Flame of Peace: A Tale of the Aztecs,* Clad Books, 1999.

Mike, Jan M. *Opossum and the Great Firemaker: A Mexican Legend.* Troll Associates, 1993.

Palacios, Argentina. *The Hummingbird King.* Troll Associates, 1993.

Parke, Marilyn and Sharon Panik. *A Quetzalcoatl Tale of the Ball Game.* Clad Books, 1999.

Shepherd, Donna Walsh. *The Aztecs.* Franklin Watts, 1992.

Wisniewski, David. *Rain Player.* Clarion Books, 1995.

Nonfiction

Bateman, Penny. *The Aztecs Activity Book.* Thames and Hudson, 1994.

Banquedano, Elizabeth. *Eyewitness. Aztec, Inca and Maya.* Dorling Kindersley Eyewitness Books, 2000.

Greene, Jacqueline D. *The Maya.* School and Library Binding, 1992.

MacDonald, Fiona. *Insights: Aztecs.* Barrons, 1993.

MacDonald, Fiona. *Step into the Aztec & Maya Worlds.* Lorenz Books, 1998.

Menchu, Rigoberta. *I...Rigoberta Menchu: An Indian Woman In Guatemala.* (trans. by Ann Wright). Verso Books, 1987.

Pitkanen, Matti A. *The Grandchildren of the Incas.* Carolrhoda Books. 1991.

Stuart, Gene S. and George E. *Lost Kingdoms of the Maya.* National Geographic Books, 1993.

Videos/Movies

A Glance at the Mexican Prehispanic Cultures. IMX, 1989.

ITV Programs. *It's Your World–Mexico.* 3 episodes, 15 minutes, KQED 1986.

National Geographic. *Lost Kingdoms of the Maya.* 60 Minutes, 1997.

Time-Life Video. (Lost Civilizations Series). *The Maya: Blood of Kings* and *The Inca: Secrets of the Ancestors.*

The Second Voyage of the Mimi (multi media program). Teacher Resources Sunburst Technology. 800-321-7511.

Hispanic Heritage poster sets, Aztec and Mayan posters, and videos from Knowledge Unlimited Inc. Call for catalog 800-356-2303.

The Walch Multicultural Art Series: *The Art of Mexico, Central America, and South America,* (77 minute video, Teacher Guide and 10 prints) J. Weston Walch Publishers.

Computer Programs

Exploring Ancient Cities CD-Rom W. H. Freeman & Company. 1994.

Exploring the Lost Maya. CD-Rom, Mac/Win Edition, Vol. 2. January 1997. Available from Educational Resources, 800-624-2926.

A Field Trip to the Rainforest. Wings for Learning, 1991.

Maya Math. (Includes teacher manual, student workbook, program disk) Sunburst Communications, 1995. Sunburst Technology. 800-321-7511.

Maya Quest. Win/Mac CD-Rom, MECC.

Internet

Maya Adventure
(ancient and modern Maya culture)
http://www.smm.org/sln/ma

The Ancient Aztecs
(in depth look at Aztec society and Spanish conquest)
http://library.thinkquest.org/27981/

Answer Key

Page 13

Food/Drinks
atole
balche
masa
pibil nal
pozole
tortillas

Plants
anona
catzim
ceiba
guano
ramon

Tools/Weapons
calabaza
curva
lelem
metates

People
padrinas
vaqueros

Miscellaneous
bravo
corrida
koben
Manhache
milpas
novenario
vigil
yuc

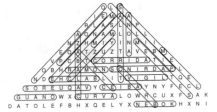

Page 14

1. j		14. g
2. d		15. b
3. w		16. a
4. s		17. v
5. f		18. u
6. n		19. y
7. k		20. i
8. o		21. l
9. h		22. c
10. e		23. p
11. t		24. r
12. x		25. q
13. m		

page 19

1. 11 Baktuns = 1,584,000
   Katuns = 93,600
   4 Unials = 4,320
   2 Kins = 2
   Total days = 1,682,002

2. 12 Baktuns = 1,728,000
   8 Katuns = 57,000
   0 Tuns = 0
   1 Unial = 20
   1 Kin = 11
   Total days = 1,785,631

page 26

1. Mexico City
2. Oaxaca
4. the national flag

page 43

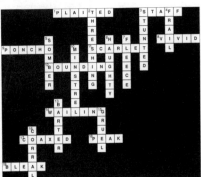

Page 46

Accept reasonable, well-thought-out answers

Page 47

The Lost City Of Machu Picchu
Lost City Found!
Lima, Peru - After years of study and research on the highly civilized Inca Empire, the American explorer Hiram Bingham headed to the jungles of the Andes Mountains in pursuit of the legendary city of Machu Pucchu. In 1911, the many difficult months of extremely hot weather, rocky terrain, and torturous vertical slopes to climb paid off for the archaeological party, as Bingham discovered the overgrown ruins of the lost city.

Though the Incas had no iron tools, weapons, or the wheel, they were able to build magnificent buildings from great stone blocks. How they moved these blocks over great distances and up the steep slopes of the Andes Mountains still remains a mystery. The city of Machu Picchu consisted of massive temples, carved buildings of white granite, courtyards, stairways and terraces. It is believed that in the 1400s, this city had been inhabited by 2,000 people.

In 1530, the Inca kingdom was invaded by Francisco Pizarro, searching for wealth and riches. The Incas were no match for the guns, cannons, horses, and diseases of the Spanish conquistadors. One brave Inca leader led a revolt and then marched a group of Indians deep into the jungles of the Andes Mountains. It was believed that this group took refuge in the fortress high in the mountains—the lost city of Machu Picchu. Today the ruins still stand as a reminder of a great people and the battle they lost.

page 51

1. a. 332 years
   b. answers will vary according to the current year, i.e. 1996–1532 = 464.

2. a. 600 tons
   b. 1600 tons
   c. 800 tons
   d. 800 tons

3. a. 30 years
   b. 11 days

page 58

1. 4
2. 7
3. 18
4. 30
5. 87
6. 360

page 62

1. j
2. d
3. f
4. h
5. b
6. i
7. e
8. c
9. a
10. g